TWICE-EXCEPTIONAL
GIFTED
CHILDREN

TWICE-EXCEPTIONAL
GIFTED
CHILDREN

Understanding, Teaching, and Counseling Gifted Students

Beverly A. Trail, Ed.D.

PRUFROCK
PRESS INC.™

PRUFROCK
ACADEMIC
PRESS

A line of materials supporting scholarship and research-based practices in education

Library of Congress Cataloging-in-Publication Data

Trail, Beverly A., 1946-
 Twice-exceptional gifted children : understanding, teaching, and counseling gifted students / by
Beverly A. Trail.
     p. cm.
Includes bibliographical references.
ISBN 978-1-59363-489-6 (pbk.)
1. Special education. 2. Gifted children--Psychology. 3. Children with disabilities--Psychology.
I. Title.
 LC3965.T678 2011
 371.95--dc22
                          2010040314

Copyright ©2011, Prufrock Press Inc.

Edited by Lacy Compton

Cover and layout design by Marjorie Parker

ISBN-13: 978-1-59363-489-6

Printed in the United States of America.

At the time of this book's publication, all facts and figures cited are the most current available; all
telephone numbers, addresses, and website URLs are accurate and active; all publications, organizations, website , and other resources exist as described in this book; and all have been verified.
The author and Prufrock Press make no warranty or guarantee concerning the information and
materials given out by organizations or content found at website , and we are not responsible for any
changes that occur after this book's publication. If you find an error or believe that a resource listed
here is not as described, please contact Prufrock Press.

Prufrock Press Inc.
P.O. Box 8813
Waco, TX 76714-8813
Phone: (800) 998-2208
Fax: (800) 240-0333
http://www.prufrock.com

CONTENTS

PREFACE

Through years of experience teaching gifted students in the public school system and working as a district gifted consultant, twice-exceptional consultant, district gifted education coordinator, and state twice-exceptional consultant/trainer, I realized that while some gifted students were achieving in school many other equally gifted students were not. I was motivated by a desire to understand the reasons why some gifted students become valedictorian of their class while other gifted students underachieve and even drop out of school. My quest to understand has resulted in a M.A. in gifted education and an Ed.D. in special education. Through this journey, I began to realize some gifted learners had significant cognitive discrepancies in their abilities. Although they had incredible strengths, these gifted learners, known as twice-exceptional learners, also had mild to moderate disabilities. When it came time to choose a topic for my doctoral dissertation, I decided to conduct a qualitative study focusing on gifted students with disabilities. The insights I gained from an extensive review of the literature and my research has helped me to gain an in-depth understanding of factors that influence the manifestation of gifted potential.

The failure of some of our most creative and brightest gifted students to develop their potential is a national tragedy. Cognitive discrepancies, asynchronous development, and unique learning styles combined with teacher's misconceptions and stereotypical notions put these gifted students at risk. Gifted students with exceptional verbal skills can have a difficult time expressing their thoughts in writing. They may be able to solve complex mathematical problems, but cannot learn the multiplication tables or pass timed skill tests. These children have knowledge of concepts well beyond their years, yet cannot complete assignments in a timely manner. Twice-exceptional learners can underachieve for years before their struggles are noticed. Unfortunately, more often than not their underachievement is attributed to lack of effort and punitive measures are implemented. As their frustration increases, social and emotional problems emerge. Behavior problems can become the focus of interventions.

This book compiles the most recent research on gifted students with disabilities into a comprehensive, easy-to-use guide. Administrators, classroom teachers, parents, and gifted and special education teachers/specialists can use this book to develop a broad understanding of the complex issues associated with gifted students who have disabilities. The chapters can guide a collaborative team step-by-step through the process of identifying student needs, selecting strategies, and developing a comprehensive plan to meet the diverse needs of twice-exceptional children.

INTRODUCTION

Twice-exceptional learners (gifted students with disabilities) continue to be a misunderstood, misjudged, and neglected segment of the student population (Bianco, 2005; Brody & Mills, 1997; Cline & Schwartz, 1999; Davis & Rimm, 2004; Karnes, Shaunessy, & Bislan, 2004; Whitmore & Maker, 1985). For years, gifted and special education students were thought to be at opposite ends of the intelligence spectrum. It was not until the 1970s that educators realized gifted students also could have disabilities. James J. Gallagher coined the term *twice-exceptional* to denote students who are both gifted and have disabilities (Coleman, Harradine, & King, 2005). Masked disabilities make aspects of academic achievement difficult for these gifted students. Identification of students who are twice-exceptional is difficult because their strengths and weaknesses mask each other, creating a unique learner profile. The profiles of twice-exceptional students are atypical of a gifted student or a student with disabilities. The educational needs of twice-exceptional students tend to be overlooked when the students are assessed for either gifted or special education services because their special characteristics are not considered in the separate identification protocols (Brody & Mills, 1997). Often the disabilities and/or gifted potential remain unnoticed for years while the student level of frustration continues to increase.

OVERVIEW OF CHAPTERS

The important concepts discussed in each chapter are summarized in the overview below. The chapters build on each other to create a comprehensive understanding of what twice-exceptional learners need in order to be successful in school.

Chapter 1: Unique Learners
- Twice-exceptional learners have the characteristics of gifted students and students with disabilities.
- There is no federal definition for twice-exceptional learners to guide the identification process.
- Unique characteristics can make it difficult for twice-exceptional learners to qualify for either gifted or special education services.
- Twice-exceptional learners are at risk when services are delayed.

Chapter 2: Response To Intervention
- Response to intervention can be effectively implemented to meet the diverse needs of twice-exceptional learners.
- It is a collaborative process involving classroom teachers, gifted education specialists, special education specialists, parents, students, and other specialists or administrators as needed.
- The problem-solving process provides a comprehensive structure to define student needs, plan interventions, implement the plan, monitor students' progress, and make sure the plan is modify accordingly.
- Tiers of interventions include specific strategies at the universal, targeted, and intensive levels.

Chapter 3: Continuum of Needs and Services
- Determine the risk and resiliency factors that are influencing the student's achievement in a positive or negative way.
- Review qualitative and quantitative data to get a clear understanding of the student's abilities and disabilities. Recommend additional assessments if needed.
- Define the individual student's strengths and challenges.

- Identify learner needs and develop measurable goals that will guide interventions.
- Provide a continuum of services to meet the diverse needs of twice-exceptional learners.
- Monitor student's progress and modify the plan to ensure the student is achieving at a level commensurate with her ability.

Chapter 4: Nurturing Gifted Potential
- Twice-exceptional learners need a supportive learning environment that values individual differences with the focus of instruction on students' strengths.
- Differentiate the curriculum to provide both challenging learning opportunities in their areas of strength and support for their deficit areas.
- Emphasize higher order thinking and problem solving to provide the challenge twice-exceptional students need to remain engaged in the learning process.
- Reduce "drill and kill" assignments and provide respectful, relevant tasks with real-world connections.

Chapter 5: Supporting Cognitive Style
- Cognitive style can contribute to the student's academic success or failure.
- Twice-exceptional learners often have a significant discrepancy between verbal and performance scores on cognitive assessments.
- Appreciably lower scores on the processing speed index is very common in twice-exceptional learners. Deficits in executive functioning skills result in problems with organization, time management, and prioritizing.
- Sensory integration issues are common when the hemispheres of the brain are not integrated.

Chapter 6: Encouraging Academic Achievement
- Twice-exceptional learners continue to be at risk in an educational system that does not understand their unique characteristics or needs.
- Underachievement is a learned behavior that is easier to prevent than to reverse once it has become chronic.
- A one-size-fits-all approach to learning does not meet the unique needs of twice-exceptional learners.
- A focus on fixing students often results in defiant behavior while an encouraging approach helps students develop the skills they need to be successful.
- Gifted students with disabilities can struggle with dyslexia, dysgraphia, and dyscalculia.

Chapter 7: Fostering Interpersonal Relationships
- Positive relationships with peers, teachers, and parents are essential for twice-exceptional learners' social and emotional development.
- Family dynamics can empower students to develop their potential or can enable them to use their disability as an excuse.
- Twice-exceptional students must be coached in developing self-advocacy skills.
- Participating in extracurricular school activities extends learning opportunities and promotes affiliations with other students who have similar interests.

Chapter 8: Promoting Intrapersonal Understanding
- Twice-exceptional learners are confused by their mixed abilities and, as a result, they experience a great deal of anxiety and depression.
- It is important for twice-exceptional learners to understand and accept their strengths and challenges.
- Dysfunctional perfectionism prevents students from viewing their accomplishments as successes.
- Learning to set realistic goals can lead to increased resiliency and self-esteem.

Chapter 9: Putting the Pieces Together
- Educational experiences, interpersonal relationships, and intrapersonal understanding directly relates to resiliency and achievement.
- Resiliency increases with supportive interpersonal relationships, positive educational experiences, and intrapersonal understanding.
- With realistic goals, internal locus of control, and the knowledge that they can be successful, twice-exceptional learners can become self-actualized.

Chapter 1

Unique Learners

Twice-exceptional learners are unique individuals with learning characteristics that are atypical of gifted students or students with disabilities. There is no federal definition to guide the identification of this special population of gifted students. As a result, misconceptions and stereotypical notions hinder the identification of twice-exceptional learners. This chapter will examine the characteristics of twice-exceptional learners and their unique learner profiles. It will scrutinize misconceptions and stereotypical beliefs that hinder identification, leaving students vulnerable in an education system that does not understand their unique needs.

CHARACTERISTICS

Twice-exceptional learners have the "characteristics of gifted students with potential for high performance, along with the characteristics of students with disabilities who struggle with many aspects of learning" (Brody & Mills, 1997, p. 282). The extremes of their abilities and disabilities can create academic, social, and emotional conflicts.

Characteristics of Gifted Learners

Typically, twice-exceptional learners have a superior vocabulary (Nielsen, 2002; Reis, Neu, & McGuire, 1995), penetrating insights into complex issues (Nielsen, 2002), and a wide range of interests (Nielsen & Higgins, 2005). They can develop consuming interests in a particular topic and develop expertise beyond their years (Nielsen, 2002). Twice-exceptional learners are highly creative (Baum & Owen, 1988; Reis et al., 1995), divergent thinkers with a sophisticated sense of humor. Their sense of humor can at times be viewed as "bizarre" (Nielsen, 2002). With other gifted students they share a propensity for advanced-level content, task commitment in areas of interest, a desire for creating original products, enjoyment of abstract concepts, and a nonlinear learning style (Renzulli, 1978; Tannenbaum & Baldwin, 1983; Van Tassel-Baska, 1991; Whitmore, 1980). They learn concepts quickly and hate "drill and practice" assignments, preferring open-ended assignments and to solve real-world problems (Baum & Owen, 1988). They have a high energy level and tend to be more interested in the "big picture" than the details. Twice-exceptional learners are curious and constantly questioning to gain a more in-depth understanding of issues and concepts.

Characteristics of Students With Disabilities

Twice-exceptional children lack the skills they need to be successful in school even though they have the characteristics of gifted students. The academic performance of twice-exceptional learners can be inconsistent with reported problems with reading, expressive language, writing, and math skills (Nielsen, 2002; Reis et al., 1995). Cognitive processing deficits in auditory processing, visual processing, and processing speed decreases their ability to process information and negatively influences their academic achievement. Lack of organizational skills results in messy desks, backpacks, lockers, and problems keeping track of papers. Deficits in prioritizing and planning make it difficult for them to complete assignments in a timely manner. They are easily distracted and experience difficulties in focusing and sustaining attention (Reis et al., 1995). Problems with gross and fine motor coordination is evidenced by poor handwriting and lack of coordination when playing sports (Weinfeld, Barnes-Robinson, Jeweler, & Shevitz, 2002). Many twice-exceptional learners experience short- and long-term memory deficits, making it difficult to memorize math facts and remember names of letters and grammar and spelling rules. They have difficulty thinking in a linear fashion and may be unable to follow directions (Nielsen, 2002).

Strengths

- superior vocabulary
- highly creative
- resourceful
- curious
- imaginative
- questioning
- problem-solving ability
- sophisticated sense of humor
- wide range of interests
- advanced ideas and opinions
- special talent or consuming interest

Challenges

- easily frustrated
- stubborn
- manipulative
- opinionated
- argumentative
- sensitive to criticism
- inconsistent academic performance
- difficulty with written expression
- lack of organization and study skills
- difficulty with social interactions

Figure 1. Frustrations result from conflicting strengths and challenges.

Social and Emotional Characteristics

Their unique characteristics can thrust twice-exceptional children into emotional frustration (Nielsen & Higgins, 2005). The extreme frustration these gifted learners feel when they cannot meet their own and others' expectations, combined with frustration of teachers who cannot understand why a bright child does not achieve, leads to conflict, misunderstandings, and failure in school. They can appear stubborn, opinionated, and argumentative, yet they also can be highly sensitive to criticism. Many twice-exceptional learners have limited interpersonal and/or intrapersonal skills (Nielsen, 2002; Reis et al., 1995) and can become the target of peer bullying, which leads to feelings of isolation when they are unable to experience normal peer relationships. In an effort to avoid failure, twice-exceptional learners may try to manipulate the situation. A refusal to complete assignments may be an attempt to avoid failure. When faced with failure, twice-exceptional learners can become very anxious, angry, and depressed.

It is the contrast between the student's abilities and disabilities that creates conflicts and tends to makes school a frustrating experience for the twice-exceptional learner, their parents, and teachers. Figure 1 provides a visual representation of the combination of contrasting strengths and challenges that creates academic, social, and emotional problems for twice-exceptional learners. Use this figure to help students, parents, and teachers understand how the strengths and challenges influence the achievement and behavior of twice-exceptional learners. Figure 2 provides a more extensive list of twice-exceptional characteristics. Copy this list and ask teachers and parents to identify specific strengths and challenges of a twice-exceptional learner. This information will be used to identify needs in the Twice-Exceptional Planning Continuum, presented later in this book.

DIFFERENT PERSPECTIVES

Historically, the academic, social, and emotional needs of twice-exceptional students have been overlooked because of stereotypical notions (Whitmore, 1981). Widespread beliefs that gifted students score uniformly high on tests of intelligence and are teacher pleasers have prevailed since the early 20th century when Lewis Terman began using the Stanford-Binet IQ test, an intelligence test, to identify students with mental retardation (now called intellectual disabilities) who would not benefit from education and to identify students with superior mental abilities (Davis & Rimm, 2004). Gifted students and students with intellectual disabilities were believed to be at opposite ends of the intellectual spectrum. The early focus of gifted education was on students with superior IQ scores and the focus of special education was on children with intellectual disabilities.

Education of Gifted Students

Early research brought empirical and scientific credibility to the field of gifted education. Terman became known as the father of gifted education for his longitudinal study of 1,528 gifted students that began in 1921. This study concluded that gifted students had superior mental abilities and were physically, psychologically, and socially healthier than their peers (Burks, Jensen, & Terman, 1930; Oden, 1968; Terman, 1925; Terman & Oden, 1947, 1959). Students were selected for the study based on their IQ scores. Davis and Rimm (2004) were critical of the selection process used for this study because classroom teachers selected the students who would participate in IQ testing. Students selected for the study were more likely to be teacher pleasers. It should be noted that two students, Luis Alvarez and William Shockley, were not included in the study because their IQ scores were not high enough, yet years later they achieved distinction as Nobel Prize winners. The description of the gifted child as the "near perfect child" is not an accurate picture of many gifted children, and it continues to place destructive internal and external pressures on students who are gifted but do not fit the perfect mold (Davis & Rimm, 2004).

The field of gifted education has experienced many ups and downs. When Russia launched the satellite Sputnik in 1957, American education was criticized

Characteristics of Twice-Exceptional Learners
Cognitive Characteristics

- Discrepancy among standardized test scores
- Superior verbal and communication skills
- Visual learner with strong perceptual reasoning skills
- High level of reasoning and problem-solving abilities
- Conceptual thinker who comprehends "big picture"
- Unable to think in a linear fashion
- Auditory processing deficits and difficulty following verbal instructions
- Slow processing speed and/or problems with fluency and automaticity
- Executive functioning deficits in planning, prioritizing, and organizing
- Highly creative, curious, and imaginative
- High energy level
- Distractible, unable to sustain attention, or problems with short-term memory
- Sensory integration issues

Academic Characteristics

- Demonstrates inconsistent or uneven academic skills
- Advanced ideas and opinions
- Wide range of interests
- Advanced vocabulary
- Penetrating insights
- Specific talent or consuming interest
- Hates drill and practice assignments
- Difficulty expressing feelings or explaining ideas or concepts
- Work can be extremely messy
- Poor penmanship and problems completing paper-and-pencil tasks
- Avoids school tasks, and frequently fails to complete assignments.
- Appears apathetic, is unmotivated, and lacks academic initiative

Interpersonal Characteristics

- Difficulty relating to peers, poor social skills, and/or antisocial behavior
- Capable of setting up situations to own advantage
- Isolated from peers and does not participate in school activities
- Target of peer bullying
- Cannot read social clues
- Lacks self-advocacy skills
- Disruptive or clowning behavior

Intrapersonal Characteristics

- Highly sensitive to criticism
- Perfectionist who is afraid to risk making a mistake
- Denies problems and/or blames others for mistakes and problems
- Believes success is due to ability or "luck"
- Behaves impulsively
- Self-critical, has low self-esteem and self-efficacy
- High levels of anxiety and/or depression
- Easily frustrated, gives up quickly on tasks

Figure 2. Characteristics of twice-exceptional learners. Adapted from Nielsen, 1993.

for the lack of challenging curriculum. According to the National Association for Gifted Children (n.d.b), this triggered an effort to improve education and paved the way for the development of challenging curriculum for gifted students who were capable of completing advanced study in math and science. Later, elitism characterized by the belief that gifted students are inherently superior led to an anti-intellectual backlash directed toward gifted education (Colangelo, 2003). Today, No Child Left Behind legislation has placed greater emphasis on students who are not performing at acceptable levels (VanTassel-Baska, 2006).

Education of Students With Disabilities

Students with intellectual disabilities were excluded from public education, forcing parents to keep their children at home or put them in an institution. In 1954, *Brown v. Board of Education* ended separate but equal education and opened the doors for similar gains by special education. Because many students with disabilities continued to be denied a public education, parents began to lobby for a free, appropriate public education (FAPE) for their children in 1960. The Elementary and Secondary Education Act (ESEA) addressed inequities of students in 1965. Congress established the Bureau for the Education of the Handicapped in 1966 with the Title VI amendment to the Elementary and Secondary Education Act (ESEA) and provided a small amount of federal funds for the education of students with disabilities.

Parents lobbied for state laws requiring local education agencies (LEAs) to provide special education services to their children with disabilities. Two federal court cases focused attention on students with disabilities. *Pennsylvania Association for Retarded Citizens (PARC) v. Commonwealth of Pennsylvania* (1971) and *Mills v. Board of Education of District of Columbia* (1972) found under the Fourteenth Amendment of the United States Constitution that it was the responsibility of state and local school districts to educate students with disabilities. The Education for the Handicapped Act (EHA) combined several initiatives to provide limited financial assistance under one law in 1972. States joined advocates to seek passage of federal legislation to subsidize the cost of special education. FAPE for special education students became a reality with the 1975 Education for All Handicapped Children Act (EAHCA). It was renamed the Individuals with Disabilities Education Act, or IDEA, in 1990. IDEA was reauthorized with substantive changes in 1997 and again in 2004.

CONVERGING IDEAS

During the 1970s, definitions of both gifted education and special education broadened. The Marland (1972) definition included intellectual, specific academic, leadership, creative and productive thinking, visual and performing arts, and psychomotor abilities. The ranks of special education were expanded to include more students with less severe disabilities. EAHCA and IDEA included students with physical, language, speech and vision, mental retardation (now considered intellectual disabilities), and emotional and behavioral disabilities. With the expanded definitions in the 1970s came the realization that gifted students could have disabilities and the categories of gifted and disabled were not mutually exclusive (Davis & Rimm, 2004; Grimm, 1998).

The Council for Exceptional Children formed a committee in 1975 to discuss twice-exceptional students (Coleman, 2005). That year, two twice-exceptional projects received federal funding. A project in Chapel Hill, NC, was based on Bloom's taxonomy and a project at the University of Illinois focused on Guilford's Structure of the Intellect (SOI). In 1976, the Council for Exceptional Children and the Connecticut Department of Education sponsored the first conference on twice-exceptionality. About this time, Maker (1977) hypothesized that the incidence of giftedness should occur at the same rate in the population of students with disabilities as it did in the population of students without disabilities. She estimated that 3% of special education students were gifted. Today, we do not know exactly how many students fall into the ranks of twice-exceptionality, but in 1993, The National Research Center on the Gifted and Talented reported that 2%–7% of the special education population was comprised of twice-exceptional learners, based on data collected by the center (see Nielsen, 1993).

In a seminal article, Whitmore (1981) indicated a new area of professional specialization was beginning. She calculated that between 120,000 and 180,000 handicapped students were gifted. However, in 1982, the U.S. Supreme Court in *Board of Education of Hendrick Hudson Central School District v. Rowley* found that Amy Rowley, a hearing impaired student, was performing adequately and progressing through the grades. The Supreme Court held that the law did not require states to develop the potential of students with disabilities (La Morte, 2005). This decision has negatively influenced the education of gifted students with disabilities and prevented students who performed at grade level from receiving special education services. From 1990–1996, the Jacob K. Javits Gifted Education Grant funded the Twice-Exceptional Child Project (Nielsen, 1989, 1993) that continues to guide the education of twice-exceptional students. In addition, Project High Hopes (Baum, 1997), funded from 1993 to 1996, focused on authentic projects and the importance of developing the strengths of twice-exceptional students.

DEFINITIONS

A clear definition of giftedness supports common understanding, while incomplete definitions can lead to misunderstandings and sporadic progress (Moon, 2006). Definitions can discriminate against students and deny services to special populations of students including minority, poor, underachieving, disabled, and gifted students (Davis & Rimm, 2004). An equitable definition of giftedness helps educators identify and serve children from a wide variety of backgrounds and cultures (Moon, 2006). Labeling students can have both positive and negative influences on expectations of others and the student's self-esteem. Being identified as gifted raises expectations while identification of a disability tends to lower teacher expectations (Bianco, 2005). To be effective, an educational definition should reflect current theory and research, be incorporated into the school's mission statement, provide the foundation for identification, and be linked to specific programming services (Moon, 2006).

Definition of Gifted Students

Researchers and theorists in gifted education seek to generate a clear definition of giftedness while our understanding of the topic continues to change (Moon, 2006). The social construct of giftedness is influenced by cultural values and politics. Lewis Terman (1925) defined giftedness as a score of more than 140 on the Stanford-Binet IQ test. The multiple intelligences theory developed by Howard Gardner (1999) and Robert Sternberg's (1985) triarchic theory are examples of neurobiological/cognitive definitions. Renzulli's (1978) three-ring conception of giftedness is a creative-productive definition utilizing multiple measures of standardized IQ tests, academic achievement tests, and authentic assessments in the identification process. Psychosocial definitions of Tannenbaum (1986) and Gagné (2000) emphasized the role of individual characteristics and environmental factors (Moon, 2006). The contemporary paradigm of gifted education recognizes diversity within the population of gifted students and a shift from psychometric perspectives to promote a multidimensional view (Bianco, 2005; Feldman, 1992).

Composite definitions are comprised of multiple theoretical perspectives and are the most widely adopted definitions by states and school districts. The Marland Report (1972) and the U.S. Department of Education's (1993) *National Excellence: A Case for Developing America's Talent* report provide examples of composite definitions. These definitions usually are operationalized with separate identification procedures for each talent area. The Marland definition was modified by Congress in 1978 and again in 1988. The federal definition reads as follows:

Children and youth with outstanding talent who perform or show the potential for performing at remarkably high levels of accomplishment when compared with others of their age, experience, or environment. These children and youth exhibit high performance capability in intellectual, creative, and/or artistic areas, possess an unusual leadership capacity, or excel in specific academic fields. They require services or activities not ordinarily provided by the schools. Outstanding talents are present in children and youth from all cultural groups across all economic strata, and in all areas of human endeavor. (U.S. Department of Education, 1993, p. 26)

The National Association for Gifted Children (n.d.c) has updated its definition of gifted children to read as follows:

A gifted person is someone who shows, or has the potential for showing, an exceptional level of performance in one or more areas of expression.
Some of these abilities are very general and can affect a broad spectrum of the person's life, such as leadership skills or the ability to think creatively. Some are very specific talents and are only evident in particular circumstances, such as a special aptitude in mathematics, science, or music. The term giftedness provides a general reference to this spectrum of abilities without being specific or dependent on a single measure or index. It is generally recognized that approximately five percent of the student population, or three million children, in the United States are considered gifted.
A person's giftedness should not be confused with the means by which giftedness is observed or assessed. Parent, teacher, or student recommendations, a high mark on an examination, or a high IQ score are not giftedness; they may be a signal that giftedness exists. Some of these indices of giftedness are more sensitive than others to differences in the person's environment. (para. 4–6)

The definition evolves as research continues and our understanding of giftedness increases. It is important to remember that gifted potential is present in students from all cultural groups and economic backgrounds. However, for gifted potential to develop, it must be nurtured. Educators play an important role in supporting the development of gifted potential. I like Renzulli's definition of giftedness, which is also on the National Association for Gifted Children's (n.d.c) website and reads as follows:

Gifted behavior occurs when there is an interaction among three basic clusters of human traits: above-average general and/or specific abilities, high levels of task commitment (motivation), and high levels of creativity. Gifted and talented children are those who possess or are capable of developing this composite of traits and applying them to any potentially valuable area of human performance. As noted in the Schoolwide Enrichment Model, gifted behaviors can be found "in certain people (not all people), at certain times (not all the time), and under certain circumstances (not all circumstances)." (para. 11)

Definition of Students With Disabilities

The Education for All Handicapped Children Act and the Individuals with Disabilities Education Act broadened the definition of children with disabilities and identified specific categories of disabilities. IDEA's definition of disability reads as follows:

> Child with a disability means a child evaluated in accordance with Sec. Sec. 300.304 through 300.311 as having mental retardation, a hearing impairment (including deafness), a speech or language impairment, a visual impairment (including blindness), a serious emotional disturbance (referred to in this part as "emotional disturbance"), an orthopedic impairment, autism, traumatic brain injury, an other health impairment, a specific learning disability, deaf-blindness, or multiple disabilities, and who, by reason thereof, needs special education and related services. (IDEA, 2004, Section 300.8)

Knoblauch and Sorenson (1998) provided a summary of the individual disability definitions under IDEA:

- **Autism:** A developmental disability significantly affecting verbal and nonverbal communication and social interaction, generally evident before age 3, that adversely affects a child's educational performance. Other characteristics often associated with autism are engagement in repetitive activities and stereotyped movements, resistance to environmental change or change in daily routines, and unusual responses to sensory experiences.
- **Deafness:** A hearing impairment so severe that the child cannot understand what is being said even with a hearing aid.
- **Deaf-Blindness:** A combination of hearing and visual impairments causing such severe communication, developmental, and educational problems that the child cannot be accommodated in either a program specifically for the deaf or a program specifically for the blind.
- **Emotional Disturbance:** A condition exhibiting one or more of the following characteristics, displayed over a long period of time and to a marked degree that adversely affects a child's educational performance:
  - An inability to learn that cannot be explained by intellectual, sensory, or health factors
  - An inability to build or maintain satisfactory interpersonal relationships with peers or teachers.
  - Inappropriate types of behavior or feelings under normal circumstances.

- A general pervasive mood of unhappiness or depression.
- A tendency to develop physical symptoms or fears associated with personal or school problems.
- This term includes schizophrenia, but does not include students who are socially maladjusted, unless they have a serious emotional disturbance.

- **Hearing impairment:** An impairment in hearing, whether permanent or fluctuating, that adversely affects a child's educational performance but that is not included under the definition of deafness as listed above.
- **Mental retardation:** Significantly subaverage general intellectual functioning existing concurrently with deficits in adaptive behavior and manifested during the developmental period that adversely affects a child's educational performance.
- **Multiple disabilities:** A combination of impairments (such as mental retardation-blindness, or mental retardation-physical disabilities) that causes such severe educational problems that the child cannot be accommodated in a special education program solely for one of the impairments. The term does not include deaf-blindness.
- **Orthopedic impairment:** A severe orthopedic impairment that adversely affects educational performance. The term includes impairments such as amputation, absence of a limb, cerebral palsy, poliomyelitis, and bone tuberculosis.
- **Other health impairment:** Having limited strength, vitality, or alertness due to chronic or acute health problems such as a heart condition, rheumatic fever, asthma, hemophilia, and leukemia, which adversely affect educational performance.
- **Specific learning disability:** A disorder in one or more of the basic psychological processes involved in understanding or in using language, spoken or written, that may manifest itself in an imperfect ability to listen, think, speak, read, write, spell, or do mathematical calculations. This term includes conditions such as perceptual disabilities, brain injury, minimal brain dysfunction, dyslexia, and developmental aphasia. This term does not include children who have learning problems that are primarily the result of visual, hearing, or motor disabilities; mental retardation; or environmental, cultural, or economic disadvantage.
- **Speech or language impairment:** A communication disorder such as stuttering, impaired articulation, language impairment, or a voice impairment that adversely affects a child's educational performance.
- **Traumatic brain injury:** An acquired injury to the brain caused by an external physical force, resulting in total or partial functional disability or psychosocial impairment, or both, that adversely affects a child's educational performance. The term applies to open or closed head inju-

ries resulting in impairments in one or more areas, such as cognition; language; memory; attention; reasoning; abstract thinking; judgment; problem-solving; sensory, perceptual, and motor abilities; psychosocial behavior; physical functions; information processing; and speech. The term does not apply to brain injuries that are congenital or degenerative, or brain injuries induced by birth trauma.

- **Visual impairment, including blindness:** An impairment in vision that, even with correction, adversely affects a child's educational performance. The term includes both partial sight and blindness. (p. 2)

The number of individuals identified with a learning disability has increased by 150%–200% since 1975 (Scruggs & Mastropieri, 2002). This has dramatically impacted school districts across the nation because the cost of educating students with disabilities is twice the cost of educating general education students (Vaughn & Fuchs, 2003). Flaws in the discrepancy method blamed for this increase include (a) the inability to distinguish if poor school performance was a result of a learning disability or underachievement, (b) statistical regression that causes scores to regress toward the mean over time, (c) overestimation and underestimate of ability, and (d) lack of sensitivity to learning problems (Fuchs, Mock, Morgan, & Young, 2003). IDEA (2004) changed the way eligibility decisions are made. Now the process is more student-centered and includes a collaborative team informed by assessment data and progress-monitoring decisions based on the student's needs and strengths (U.S. Department of Education, n.d.).

Definition of Twice-Exceptional Students

There is no federal definition for twice-exceptional students and the lack of a clear description has resulted in only a limited number of gifted students with disabilities being identified (Brody & Mills, 1997). Many states and school districts require twice-exceptional students to meet the eligibility criteria for both giftedness and disabilities.

Using separate definitions for giftedness and disabilities is problematic. Gifted learners with disabilities frequently do not meet the identification criteria for either exceptionality because gifted characteristics can mask the disability and the disability can mask the giftedness (Maker & Udall, 1985). A definition for twice-exceptional learners could read as follows:

Twice-exception learners have the characteristics of gifted students and students with disabilities. They have the potential for exceptional performance in one or more areas of expression, which includes general areas such as creativity and leadership or specific areas such as math, science, and music. These students have an accompanying disability in one or more of categories defined by IDEA.

Comprehensive educational planning by a collaborative team is necessary for meeting twice-exceptional learners' diverse needs. These students need a continuum of services to nurture their gifted potential, to provide support in their area(s) of disability, to foster positive interpersonal relationships, and to promote intrapersonal understanding.

IDENTIFICATION

Early identification and appropriate interventions can help to prevent the development of social and behavioral problems that can occur when the needs of a gifted child with learning disabilities are overlooked (Brody & Mills, 1997; Whitmore, 1980). Yet, the identification of twice-exceptional learners continues to be problematic because of ambiguities related to the definitions for giftedness and disabilities (Hannah & Shore, 1995). Twice-exceptional learners are a heterogeneous group representing all types of giftedness combined with various disabilities (Brody & Mills, 1997). There is no consensus on one defining pattern or set of scores to identify gifted students with disabilities. Identifying students for gifted programs and students with disabilities for special education services continue to be mutually exclusive activities (Boodoo, Bradley, Frontera, Pitts, & Wright, 1989). Relying on separate prevailing definitions and identification procedures for gifted students and students with disabilities makes identification difficult when students possess characteristics of both groups. The separate protocols used to identify students for gifted and special education fail to consider the unique characteristics of students with both exceptionalities. Atypical learning styles and rigid cut-off scores make it difficult for these students to qualify for either gifted or special education programming (Trail, 2006).

The early struggles of twice-exceptional students often go unnoticed when the gifted characteristics mask the disability and the disability masks the gifted potential. Some will be identified as gifted, others as students with disabilities, and many will not receive any services because they appear to be average students. Twice-exceptional children can reach developmental milestones before their age peers. Their advanced vocabulary and communication skills raise teachers' and parents' expectations for achievement in school. As they progress through the grades, they begin to experience difficulties in school. Twice-exceptional learners work hard to hide their learning problems and to maintain the persona of a gifted student. However, each year it becomes harder for these students to maintain their gifted identity. Because their learning problems remain unrecognized, their achievement continues to decline. These students often become known as underachievers and unmotivated students and, sometimes, less-flattering terms such as lazy are used to describe them (Silverman, 1993). By the time their performance drops below grade level and someone suspects a disability, their gifted potential may no longer be visible.

Stereotypical beliefs can hinder the identification of twice-exceptional children (Bianco, 2005; Cline & Hedgeman, 2001; Johnson, Karnes, & Carr, 1997; Whitmore & Maker, 1985). Gifted potential is seldom identified in students with failing grades and incomplete assignments (King, 2005). Some educators question if a student with serious learning problems can be gifted (Brody & Mills, 1997). Research by Bianco (2005) found that once a child was identified with a disability, teachers were reluctant to refer him for gifted programming. Gifted students with emotional and behavior problems often are not referred for gifted programs or they are terminated from gifted programs because of their behavior (Reid & McGuire, 1995). Unfortunately, too many twice-exceptional students fail to meet the eligibility requirements for either giftedness or learning disabilities because identification protocols fail to consider the special characteristics of this population (Brody & Mills, 1997). Time and energy is wasted determining if students are truly gifted and/or if they qualify for special education services. Many twice-exceptional learners who are not identified for services provided by gifted education or special education are later identified for personality and behavioral problems (Waldron, Saphire, & Rosenblum, 1987).

Evidence of underachievement typically is required in screening for learning disabilities (Beckley, 1998). Gifted students rarely get referred because they are able to compensate for their learning problems (Senf, 1983). Although they may be underachieving when compared to their potential, their above-grade-level performance can prevent their identification for a learning problem. The criteria for identifying students with a learning disability in some states requires achievement to be at least 2 years below grade level in at least one subject area. Therefore, it is unlikely that a young gifted student with learning disabilities will be identified (Reis & McCoach, 2002). Many educators view below-grade-level achievement as a prerequisite to a diagnosis of a learning disability (Baum, 1990). Even when teachers recognize the student has issues that would lead them to believe there is a disability, the determination that a student is not eligible for special services means they will remain in the general education program (Reid & McGuire, 1995). Selecting students whose achievement is in the bottom 20% of the class for intervention will mean that gifted students with learning disabilities, who function at or near grade level, will not be identified. Achievement of gifted students must be compared to their ability (Reynolds, Zetlin, & Wang, 1993; Siegel & Metsala, 1992). Evidence of a processing deficit can be helpful in differentiating between a gifted learner who is underachieving and a gifted learner with a disability (Rimm, 1986; Whitmore & Maker, 1985). Distinguishing underachievement from learning problems caused by neurological dysfunction is important to maintain integrity in the field of learning disabilities (Adelman, 1992). Twice-exceptional students can underachieve for many years before their achievement falls significantly below the average level of their age peers. In fact, some students are never identified for either gifted or special education programming.

New Directions

The Individuals with Disabilities Education Improvement Act (IDEA) of 2004 and the Response to Intervention (RtI) model reflect new ideas related to the way educators assess, identify, and provide services to students with disabilities. The reauthorization of IDEA mentioned gifted students with disabilities for the first time as a priority group whose needs can be funded in U.S. Department of Education grants for research, personnel preparation, and technical assistance. This is a major step forward in advocating for the needs of twice-exceptional students (Coleman et al., 2005). Another important provision of IDEA is the change in the way educators identify students with learning disabilities. The presence of a disability will be determined by how a child responds to scientific research-based interventions (Graner, Faggella-Luby, & Fritschmann, 2005). RtI is alleviating many of the current concerns related to the IQ discrepancy model. The focus of RtI is on results and outcomes, not eligibility and process. Students do not have to qualify for special education services before interventions can begin. Interventions can begin as soon as data analysis shows the student is not progressing adequately. No longer will students have to "wait-to-fail" before qualifying for special education services. Response to Intervention is currently being successfully implemented in many states to meet the needs of gifted and twice-exceptional learners as well as students with disabilities.

Summary

Twice-exceptional learners have the characteristics of both gifted students and students with disabilities. Gifted characteristics can mask disabilities and/or the disability can mask the gifted potential so these students appear to have average performance. Stereotypical notions continue to cause twice-exceptional learners to be underserved in an education system that does not understand their needs. These unique learners require support from both gifted and special education specialists in order to achieve their potential. However, identification is problematic because their unique characteristics are atypical of a gifted student and a student with disabilities. With no federal definition, the needs of twice-exceptional students often are overlooked. Response to Intervention is changing the way schools provide services for students with exceptionalities. Chapter 2 will discuss in greater depth the implementation of RtI and how the collaborative problem-solving approach can challenge and support the cognitive, academic, social, and emotional needs of twice-exceptional students.

Chapter 2

RESPONSE TO INTERVENTION

Response to Intervention (RtI) is changing the way schools respond to students who are struggling to learn. Educators are encouraged to intervene earlier on behalf of a greater number of children who are at risk for school failure. RtI gives educators a process for determining whether a child responds to evidence-based interventions and deciding which students need more intensive levels of intervention. RtI emphasizes research-based quality instruction, continuous monitoring of student progress, early intervention for students who are at risk of academic failure, and evidence-based interventions with increasing intensity at higher levels. In particular, the focus on research-based quality instruction will decrease the number of students who are not achieving because of poor instruction rather than an inherent disability (Fuchs & Fuchs, 2005). The systematic approach used by RtI ensures that at-risk students receive timely and effective support when they first begin to experience academic difficulties. No longer will students have to wait to fail before they can qualify for services.

The Association for the Gifted, a division of the Council for Exceptional Children (2009), and the National Association for Gifted Children (n.d.a) recommended in position statements the expansion of RtI to include gifted and twice-exceptional learners. The implementation of RtI throughout the country is substantially impacting identification and services for students with disabilities. RtI specifically addresses the needs of students who are not making adequate progress in school. It is a schoolwide initiative designed to meet the needs of all students, which should include gifted and twice-exceptional learners. This chapter will examine how the RtI multilevel system and the collaborative problem-solving approach can provide the challenge and support necessary to meet the needs of twice-exceptional learners.

Essential Components

Educating students with exceptional needs requires the implementation of programming components to meet their diverse abilities. Universal screenings, systematic assessments, and monitoring of students' progress leads to more effective and earlier identification of those who are at risk of academic failure. Twice-exceptional learners need early interventions for their disabilities and, at the same time, they need interventions that provide additional challenge in their area of giftedness. The components of RtI provide an opportunity to identify gifted students who need additional challenge in order to develop their potential. Gifted education and special education specialists could work with the classroom teacher to implement differentiated instruction.

As educators monitor behavior and implement RtI interventions, they are realizing the relationship between social and emotional needs and students' behavior. Supporting the social and emotional needs of students is equally important, but an often-neglected component in student success. Students who are experiencing social difficulties with personal relationships or showing signs of emotional distress need early intervention and support. Research demonstrates the important role interpersonal relationships and intrapersonal understanding have in student achievement and satisfaction with life (Trail, 2008). Systematic screening to identify students who were experiencing problems with social (interpersonal relationships) or emotional (intrapersonal understanding) areas would result in earlier interventions and, therefore, fewer behavior problems.

Gifted and special education specialists could provide valuable assistance to classroom teachers in addressing the needs of a wider range of students. As universal screening data is reviewed, the needs of all students would be considered. Those students needing additional challenge would be identified as well as students who were not achieving academically or had behavioral issues. As members of the collaborative problem-solving team, both specialists play a vital role in identifying student needs, selecting interventions, and developing an individual plan for students. The additional support teachers receive from such specialists is beneficial as they implement the plan and monitor student progress. The student's response to the interventions implemented determines the levels of support and tiers of intervention needed to develop their potential further.

PROFESSIONAL DEVELOPMENT

In order for any initiative to be successful in its implementation, adequate professional development is necessary. High-quality staff development builds on collaborative reflection and joint action. Schools should provide training for collaborative groups comprised of classroom teachers, gifted and special education specialists, parents, and other specialists such as school psychologists, counselors, behavior specialists, occupational therapists, and administrators. The training should focus on the unique characteristics of twice-exceptional learners, utilizing the RtI problem-solving process to identify diverse needs, select specific interventions to meet those needs, develop a comprehensive plan, and monitor student progress. Allow ample time for the collaborative teams to discuss, reflect, and apply the information they have learned to case studies of students and then to specific students in their schools. In between the training, the teams should have time for implementation and experimentation of the principles they have learned. Follow-up trainings should include reflection on the progress they have made, student successes, and the problems they have encountered. This guided implementation will lead to the best results for twice-exceptional learners.

COLLABORATION

Classroom teachers need support from both gifted and special educators as well as other education specialists to address the diverse needs of twice-exceptional learners. Research found that the best results are achieved when an individualized plan was developed through a collaborative team effort involving a gifted education specialist, special education specialist, school psychologist, classroom teacher, parents, and the student (Baum, Owen, & Dixon, 1991; VanTassel-Baska, 1991). Occasionally, administrators, counselors, social workers, and occupational or physical therapists are included on the team. The collaborative team members share their expertise as they identify students' needs, determine the level of support students need, select research-based interventions, assist teachers in developing and implementing a plan, and monitor students' progress. The collective knowledge of the team members increases the likelihood that the plan will be successful in meeting the students' needs. The expertise of each member strengthens the RtI process. The role of each member is summarized below:

Administrator
- Create a positive learning environment that recognizes that students have varied learning needs.
- Set the stage for implementing educational improvements by keeping up-to-date on the latest educational research.
- Provide professional development opportunities for staff members and work with parent organizations to provide training for parents.
- Utilize student assessment data to determine students' needs and use this information to guide instruction.
- Encourage collaboration between classroom teachers, specialists, and parents.
- Play a leading role in conflict resolution by communicating with all parties involved to resolve the issues.
- Provide the financial and educational resources teachers need to be successful.

Classroom Teacher
- Work collaboratively with the gifted education specialist, special education specialist, and other specialists to develop a comprehensive plan for meeting the needs of gifted students, twice-exceptional students, and students with disabilities.
- Utilize student data to guide instruction and ensure students are challenged at an appropriate level.
- Know the parameters of students' Individual Education Programs (IEPs) for special and/or gifted education and 504 Plans. An IEP is mandated by IDEA for students with disabilities. Some states mandate IEPs for gifted students. The 504 Plan refers to Section 504 of the Rehabilitation Act of 1973. It spells out modifications and accommodations students with disabilities need in order to perform at a comparable level to their peers.
- Differentiate classroom instruction to meet individual students' needs and improve educational outcomes for students.
- Consistently monitor the progress of students to identify (a) students who are struggling and (b) students who have learned concepts and need additional challenge.
- Implement evidence-based strategies as needed to promote students' success. Focus on students' strengths and interests.
- Support social and emotional needs of students and consult with a specialist when additional assistance is needed.

Gifted Education Specialist
- Work collaboratively with classroom teachers to analyze assessment data and identify academic, social, and emotional needs of gifted students. Assist classroom teachers in differentiating the curriculum to meet students' needs.
- Advocate for underachieving gifted students and twice-exceptional learners by providing information so teachers will understand why some gifted students do not achieve.
- Collaborate with classroom teachers, the special education team, school psychologists, social workers, counselors, occupational therapists, other specialists, and parents to develop an IEP for twice-exceptional learners.
- Focus on developing the potential of gifted and twice-exceptional learners by using challenging curriculum, strategies to promote higher level thinking, and real-life problem solving instead of providing more of the same.
- Provide opportunities for gifted and twice-exceptional learners to work with peers of similar ability and interests.

Special Education Specialist
- Work collaboratively with classroom teachers to analyze assessment data and identify learning struggles. Assist them in differentiating the curriculum to meet the needs of students with disabilities and twice-exceptional students.
- Advocate for students with disabilities and twice-exceptional learners by providing information to teachers so they will understand the students' disabilities and the effects they have on the students' achievement.
- Collaborate with classroom teachers, gifted education specialists, school psychologists, social workers, counselors, occupational therapists, other specialists, and parents to develop an individualized plan for twice-exceptional learners.
- Assist parents and students in understanding their disabilities, and help students develop compensatory strategies and utilize technology to improve performance.
- Provide explicit instruction on prioritizing, managing assignments, and time management and organizational skills so students will develop needed executive functioning skills.

School Psychologist, Counselor, and/or Social Worker
- Monitor social skill development and assist students in developing appropriate social skills.
- Facilitate the development of socials skills needed to establish and maintain friendships.

- Assist students in learning techniques they can use to approach teachers and become self-advocates.
- Monitor the emotional status of students and provide counseling as needed related to issues of perfectionism, anxiety, stress, depression, self-esteem, and suicide.
- Assist students in developing an understanding and appreciation of their strengths and challenges.

Occupational and/or Physical Therapist
- Monitor physical development and assist students in developing strategies to overcome their deficits in motor learning and coordination.
- Provide support for students with dysgraphia.
- Offer expertise in issues related to sensory integration and recommend research-based interventions as needed.

HOME-SCHOOL PARTNERSHIP

When educators and parents work together they can transform a child's educational experience (Muscott et al., 2008). Parents can provide valuable insights, because they know their child's strengths, interests, and challenges. They often notice a change in their child's behavior, signaling that something is wrong, before the problem is evident to teachers. Home-school partnerships positively influence attendance, homework completion, and achievement (Henderson, Johnson, Mapp, & Davies, 2006).

Misunderstandings can strain relationships and derail the home-school partnership. School can be a very frustrating experience for twice-exceptional children who have discrepant abilities. For a time they are able to hide their learning difficulties from peers and teachers. However, their behavior at home can indicate a serious problem before it is evident at school. Teachers may not recognize the gifted potential of a child with an undiagnosed disability because the disability masks the gifted potential. To the teacher the child may appear to be just an average student. Although it is easy to understand why a teacher might dismiss parents' concerns, it is difficult for parents to watch helplessly as their children's achievement declines and they disengage from school. Delays in identification and interventions can lead to conflicts between parents and educators. Parents become increasingly frustrated when their concerns are ignored or trivialized. The parents of twice-exceptional learners often are twice-exceptional themselves and have experienced some of the same issues. Memories of negative school experiences increase the parents' determination to make sure their children do not suffer the same fate. These parents can become very demanding and the ensuing battle can be costly for the school, parents, and students.

The following suggestions can be implemented to improve the home-school partnership:

School's Role
- Welcome parent participation in school activities, get to know their strengths, engage them in volunteering at school, and value their contributions to increase educational opportunities for students.
- Work to establish and sustain respectful relationships with parents through two-way communication and shared decision making.
- Assess parent needs and provide the support necessary for them to become partners in facilitating their children's academic progress.
- Listen carefully to parents' concerns and encourage their collaboration in the problem-solving process. Never trivialize or dismiss parents' concerns. Take the time to adequately assess students' abilities to determine if there is a hidden disability.
- Understand the frustration parents of twice-exceptional children experience when their gifted children fail in school. Recognize that some parents also may be twice-exceptional and have had negative school experiences.

Parent's Role
- Value your children's strengths, share in their passions, and model positive ways of dealing with stress and life's challenges.
- Empower your children to develop compensatory strategies for dealing with their disabilities.
- Advocate for your children, but do not rescue them from problems or demand special treatment.
- Encourage your children to become self-sufficient and to learn self-advocacy skills.
- Share your concerns with your children's teachers and help educators to understand issues that are negatively influencing your children's academic achievement.
- Work collaboratively with educators in the problem-solving process, support the implementation of recommended interventions, and utilize suggested strategies at home.
- Seek community organizations and resources to extend educational opportunities outside of school and provide opportunities for your children to work with other students with similar interests and abilities.

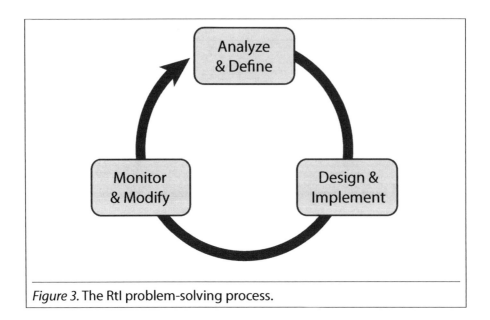

Figure 3. The RtI problem-solving process.

THE RTI PROBLEM-SOLVING PROCESS

RtI utilizes a structured, systematic problem-solving process illustrated in Figure 3. The problem-solving process is a continuous cycle of the following steps for each individual student:

- Analyze the data to determine what is keeping a student from making adequate progress.
- Define the student's academic, social, and emotional needs.
- Design a collaborative plan of interventions to meet the student's needs.
- Implement the plan with fidelity.
- Monitor the student's progress to determine the need for more or less intensive interventions.
- Modify the plan and continue to monitor the student's progress.

The various steps are explained in more detail in the sections that follow.

Analyze and Define

The referring teacher and/or parent initiates the problem-solving process. During the initial consultation, the referring teacher meets with the twice-exceptional consultant and/or the gifted and special education specialist to review the assessment data as a team. A combination of both quantitative and qualitative data is required to provide a comprehensive view of the student. After analyzing the data, the team determines if additional information or assessments are needed to gain a complete understanding of the student's strengths and challenges. The data may include a combination of any of the following: screening, diagnostic, curriculum-based, achievement, and cognitive assessments; observations; rating scales; portfolios; and interviews with the teacher, parent, and student. After the data are analyzed the problem-solving team determines the student's strengths and challenges and defines the student's academic, social, and emotional needs.

Design and Implement

The problem-solving team works collaboratively to develop a comprehensive plan of interventions that will support and challenge the student. The team is comprised of the referring teacher, twice-exceptional consultant, special education specialist, gifted education specialist, parents, and the student (the student's participation in the process will vary with the student's age and maturity level). A school counselor, social worker, reading specialist, speech/language specialist, occupational therapist, physical therapist, and an administrator may be included based on the student's needs. A home-school partnership increases the chances for success because parents and educators are working together to develop appropriate learning opportunities/interventions at home and school. The comprehensive plan the team develops should provide (a) challenging learning opportunities in areas of the student's strengths; (b) explicit instruction and support in the student's areas of challenge; and if necessary (c) foster interpersonal relationships; and (d) promote intrapersonal understanding. The team identifies the intensity and duration of the intervention. A person is designated to be responsible for implementing the intervention and monitoring the student's progress. The team then works to ensure the plan is implemented with fidelity.

Monitor and Modify

The student's progress is monitored at designated intervals throughout the year. Data from multiple sources will determine the effectiveness of the intervention. The data suggest whether (a) the intervention plan was implemented with fidelity; (b) the plan is achieving the desired results; and (c) the defined academic and affective needs were met. The team meets on a predetermined date to evaluate the student's progress. Decisions are made based on the progress of the student to either (a) maintain interventions, (b) discontinue interventions, or (c) provide more or less intensive interventions. Modifications are made to ensure the student is making adequate progress and is achieving at a level commensurate with his or her ability. Students who are not making adequate progress at the universal level receive small-group interventions and their progress monitoring continues at the targeted level. Those who do not respond to small-group interventions will receive more individualized, intensive interventions based on the tiers described in the next section.

Tiers of Intervention

There are many possible variations to the RtI model, but typically it has tiers of intervention with the intensity of the interventions increasing at each tier (Fuchs & Fuchs, 2005; Graner et al., 2005). Some states have adopted models with distinctive tiers while other states have used a more fluid approach. In the beginning the RtI tiers provided levels of intervention to support students who were not achieving in reading. The intervention tiers were later expanded to other academic areas. When RtI was adopted by special education, the model was expanded to include academic and behavior issues. Here, I have adapted the RtI model to meet the diverse needs of twice-exceptional learners.

Tier 1: Universal Interventions

The first tier focuses on providing high-quality education and differentiated instruction in the general classroom. Assessment, instruction, and monitoring student progress in this tier are the responsibility of the classroom teacher. Highly qualified teachers receive rigorous professional development so they can effectively implement evidence-based curriculum. All students are screened early in the school year to identify individuals who need additional support to meet grade-level standards and those who have already mastered aspects of the grade-level content. Teachers recognize that students learn differently and differentiate instruction according to students' readiness, interests, and learning profiles. Differentiated instruction reflects sound instructional principles and best practices. It provides the support students need to be successful and the challenge they need to keep engaged in the learning process.

Throughout the year, curriculum-based assessments supply data teachers can use to monitor students' individual progress. Diagnostic assessments provide specific information to identify skill deficits and strengths. Longitudinal growth data track the students' academic growth and are valuable in determining if students are achieving a year's growth. Although some students will not achieve a year's growth unless they receive additional support to learn grade-level material, others have already mastered parts or the entire grade-level curriculum. Gifted learners will need additional challenge in order for them to continue to grow commensurate with their ability. Twice-exceptional learners need both support in deficit areas and additional enrichment in their strength areas.

In this tier, teachers understand that interpersonal relationships and intrapersonal understanding influence student achievement and strive to provide a respectful learning environment that values individual differences and learning styles. Every student should be valued for the contributions she makes to the classroom. Teachers must support feelings of empathy and guard against peer bullying and an anti-intellectual climate. At the same time, they should provide opportunities for students to work with peers who have similar interests and abilities, encouraging students to become involved in school clubs and extracurricular activities. Teachers also must monitor the progress of students who are experiencing difficulties with interpersonal relationships and students who are anxious, depressed, or have low self-esteem.

Tier 2: Targeted Interventions

Students are identified for targeted interventions if they are (a) not progressing adequately in the regular classroom, (b) in need of additional challenge, (c) experiencing difficulties with interpersonal relationships, or (d) showing signs of emotional distress. Twice-exceptional learners have very diverse needs that must be considered when developing an instructional and intervention plan. Focusing only on deficit areas with the intent of fixing students often results in less positive outcomes of depression, lack of motivation, and loss of self-esteem. For this reason it is advantageous for classroom teachers to work collaboratively with specialists from special and gifted education to develop a comprehensive plan of evidence-based instruction and intervention.

Tier 2 evidence-based instruction and interventions are provided in small, flexible groupings within the classroom and across grade levels or pull-out groups. This allows teachers to work with small groups of students where they can focus instruction on individual needs. Small-group instruction affords twice-exceptional students an opportunity to develop higher order thinking skills, problem-solving skills, and research skills while they gain organizational skills or develop fluency skills in other groups. Pull-out friendship groups are valuable in teaching students specific social skills to improve their relationships with peers. Interest groups allow students to explore an area of interest with other students who have similar interests. Twice-exceptional learners can benefit from activities designed to increase awareness and acceptance of strengths and weaknesses. Studying famous people with disabilities is helpful because it helps twice-exceptional learners understand how others have overcome their disabilities and contributed to society. Teachers can coach students in developing realistic long-term goals and in breaking the goal into doable short-term goals. Achieving short-term goals increases the student's self-esteem. As teachers implement these strategies, the student's progress is monitored to determine if the interventions are working. If the student continues to need additional challenge, academic support in deficit areas, and help with problems with personal relationships, or if he is showing signs of emotional distress, he is referred for the intensive interventions at Tier 3.

Tier 3: Intensive Interventions

A collaborative team composed of the classroom teacher, gifted and special education specialists, parents, the student, and other education specialists begin the problem-solving process. The team collects qualitative and quantitative data and uses it to make instructional/intervention decisions. They identify the student's strength and weaknesses, and the variables that are influencing the student's achievement. A comprehensive plan of evidence-based interventions is developed, the plan is implemented with fidelity, and the student's progress is monitored to ensure his needs are being met. The formal special education eligibility evaluation begins when it is determined that more intensive interventions are necessary for the student to be successful. Parents are informed of their due process rights and procedural safeguards specified in IDEA are followed. For twice-exceptional learners it is extremely important to develop a comprehensive plan that addresses their cognitive and academic needs as gifted students and students with disabilities, as well as their social and emotional needs.

Tiers of Intervention for Twice-Exceptional Learners

Possible interventions for twice-exceptional learners to meet their academic, social, and emotional needs are shown in Figure 4. Increasingly, intervention specialists are finding a link between underachievement and behavioral issues. Likewise, behavioral interventions are more successful when the social and emotional needs of the students are considered. Behavioral interventions for twice-exceptional learners include strategies to address their social needs for interpersonal relationships with peers, parents, and teachers and their emotional needs related to intrapersonal understanding.

SUMMARY

Response to Intervention is changing the way the educational needs of students with disabilities and gifted students are identified for interventions. No longer will students with disabilities have to wait to fail before they receive the interventions and supports they need to become successful learners. Early interventions could reduce the frustration these students experience and prevent the social and emotional issues that can develop when they fail to meet their own expectations and the expectations of others. Professional collaboration between classroom teachers, gifted education specialists, and special education specialists are necessary to differentiate the instruction and develop interventions to meet the diverse needs of twice-exceptional learners. A home-school partnership is essential to provide the support at home and in the classroom that twice-exceptional learners need to be successful. Chapter 3 will provide a structured approach that can be used to develop an individualized plan for twice-exceptional learners.

Tier 1: Universal Level Interventions for Twice-Exceptional Learners

- The universal level focuses on what is happening in the general classroom.
- It seeks to ensure that all students receive high-quality differentiated instruction, taught by "highly qualified" teachers, using evidence-based curriculum and instructional practices.
- Universal screening, diagnostic assessments, and progress monitoring are used to guide instruction and intervention decisions.
- Students are referred for targeted interventions when they are:
  » not progressing adequately in the regular classroom,
  » in need of additional challenge,
  » experiencing difficulty with personal relationships, or
  » showing signs of emotional distress.

Academic Interventions		Behavioral Interventions	
Interventions to Support Academic Achievement	Interventions to Nurture Gifted Potential	Interventions to Foster Interpersonal Relationships	Interventions to Promote Intrapersonal Understanding
• Universal screening and progress monitoring to identify those at risk • Student referral for targeted interventions before they experience significant failure • Preassessment to design instruction • Differentiated curriculum, instruction, and assessment • Implementation of evidence-based interventions including flexible grouping • Choice in assignments so students can use their strengths to demonstrate what they have learned • Monitoring of student progress to document growth and make sure all students are developing needed skills	• Universal screening and progress monitoring to determine those students who need additional challenge • Preassessment to design instruction • Differentiated curriculum, instruction, and assessment • Implementation of research-based interventions including flexible grouping, faster-paced instruction, and opportunities to explore issues in greater depth and complexity • Choice in assignments that allows students to explore areas of interest and become the class expert • Monitoring of student progress to document growth and make sure each student is experiencing a year's growth	• Universal screening and progress monitoring to identify those students who are having problems with interpersonal relationships • Respectful environment that values individual differences • Guards against peer bullying and anti-intellectual climate • Supportive, encouraging teachers • Opportunities to work with peers with similar interests and abilities • Involvement in school clubs and interest groups • Monitoring to make sure students are developing social skills	• Universal screening and progress monitoring to identify those students who have discrepancy in skills and performance, low self-esteem, dysfunctional perfectionism, unrealistic expectations, anxiety, or depression • Individual differences and learning styles valued • Facilitation of understanding of personal strengths, interests, and weaknesses • Encouragement of feelings of empathy • Development of positive self-esteem • Monitoring of students who are at risk of anxiety, depression, or low self-esteem

Figure 4. Interventions for twice-exceptional learners at each tier of RtI.

Figure 4, continued

Tier 2 : Targeted Interventions for Twice-Exceptional Learners

- Supplemental instruction and interventions are implemented when the student begins to struggle and include:
  - » small-group instruction, and
  - » lower student-teacher ratio.
- Evidence-based high-quality instruction and interventions are matched to learner's needs.
- Flexible grouping within classroom or across grade level(s) and pull-out classes are use for supplemental instruction.
- Universal screening, diagnostic assessments, and progress monitoring are used to guide instruction and intervention decisions.
- The student progresses to intensive interventions of Tier 3 if they are:
  - » not progressing adequately,
  - » in need of additional challenge,
  - » experiencing difficulty with personal relationships, or
  - » showing signs of emotional distress.

Academic Interventions		Behavioral Interventions	
Interventions to Support Academic Achievement	**Interventions to Nurture Gifted Potential**	**Interventions to Foster Interpersonal Relationships**	**Interventions to Promote Intrapersonal Understanding**
• Systematic assessments and progress monitoring • Flexible grouping for instruction within classroom and across grade levels • Collaborative planning with gifted and special education specialists to implement evidence-based instruction and interventions • Supplemental instruction for a specific length of time, intensity, and duration • Evidence-based interventions to help students develop fluency and automaticity • Skill development in prioritizing, organization, study skills, and time management	• Systematic assessment and progress monitoring • Flexible grouping for instruction within classroom and across grade levels • Focus on developing individual strengths and interests • Collaborative planning with gifted education specialist to design and implement strength-based challenges • Implementation of evidence-based interventions such as small-group instruction, pull-out programs, and small-group or independent study projects • Honors and AP classes • Emphasis on critical and creative thinking and problem solving	• Systematic assessment and progress monitoring • Friendship groups to aid students in developing social skills, peer relationships, and maintaining friendships • Instruction on self-advocacy skills • Family assistance in learning to empower verses enable children • Opportunities to work with intellectual peers • Affiliations in extracurricular activities encouraged • Referrals of students who are showing signs of isolation to group counseling	• Systematic assessment and progress monitoring • Development of personal awareness, understanding, and acceptance • Understanding that success is a result of effort rather than ability • Rubrics utilized and process of self-evaluation facilitated • Coaching for students in learning to set realistic long-term goals and to break these goals into short-term goals • Celebration of attainment of individual goals and self-actualization

Figure 4, continued

Tier 3: Intensive Interventions for Twice-Exceptional Learners

- A collaborative team uses the problem-solving approach to define the problem and to identify the variables that are contributing to the problem.
- A comprehensive plan is developed by the team to address the student's cognitive, academic, social, and emotional needs.
- Diagnostic assessments and progress monitoring are used to determine if students are making adequate progress.
- Assessment data guides instructional and intervention decisions.
- Intensive interventions include:
  - » small-group and individualized instruction and interventions,
  - » formal identification for special education services, and
  - » procedural safeguards as required by IDEA 2004.

Academic Interventions		Behavioral Interventions	
Interventions to Support Academic Achievement	Interventions to Nurture Gifted Potential	Interventions to Foster Interpersonal Relationships	Interventions to Promote Intrapersonal Understanding
• Collaborative problem solving used to design and implement evidence-based instruction and interventions • Intensive, systematic specialized instruction and interventions • Formal and individualized special education eligibility evaluation • Parents informed of due process rights • Procedural safeguards as required by IDEA 2004 • Systematic assessments and progress monitoring	• Evidence-based interventions that include acceleration, dual enrollment, radical acceleration, or early college entrance • Magnet classrooms and schools designed for gifted students • Independent study projects to give students an opportunity to study a topic in greater depth. • Coaching for students in developing the habits of mind of practicing professionals • Apprenticeships to enable students to gain real-world experiences • Mentors to provide valuable guidance	• Opportunities to work with intellectual peers • Specialized counseling is necessary to assist student in dealing with intensities, sensitivities, feelings of being different, and isolation • Explicit instruction to help students improve relationships with peers, teachers, and family. • Teaching of skills students need to become self-advocates • Facilitation of mentorships and/or apprenticeships	• Specialized counseling for students who are exhibiting signs of anxiety, dysfunctional perfectionism, depression, stress, or suicidal tendencies • Assistance for students in gaining awareness, understanding, and acceptance of their strengths and challenges • Studies of famous people with similar disabilities • Development of self-regulation, locus of control, and attainment of personal goals • Teaching of coping strategies

Chapter 3

CONTINUUM OF NEEDS
AND SERVICES

Twice-exceptional learners are at risk in an educational system that does not recognize their unique characteristics or provide the timely support they need to be successful. The combination of the two exceptionalities makes it difficult for twice-exceptional students to be successful in school. Asynchronous development, a term used to describe the discrepancies between their abilities (Silverman, 1993), is one of the reasons these students are so misunderstood. Intellectual skills may be in the advanced range while motor and social skills are not as well developed. These discrepancies can intensify social and emotional issues (Schiff, Kaufman, & Kaufman, 1981; Silverman, 2002). Research conducted by Baum and Owen (1988) found that gifted students with disabilities had a heightened sense of inefficacy in school. Twice-exceptional students are internally motivated, yet they fail repeatedly because of their disability (King, 2005). This chapter will examine risk and resiliency factors that influence student achievement. It will focus on developing a comprehensive plan that decreases risk and increases resiliency by providing the challenge and support twice-exceptional learners need to achieve their full potential.

RISK AND RESILIENCY

In order to influence outcomes for students it becomes important to look at factors that place students at risk for school failure and resiliency factors that enable a student to overcome risk and adversity.

Risk Factors

Biological, psychological, cognitive, or environmental factors that hinder normal development and make students more vulnerable to negative life outcomes are referred to as risk factors (Dole, 2000). Learning disabilities are considered an adverse condition in which the child initially has little control (Spekman, Goldberg, & Herman, 1993). It increases their vulnerability to distorted perceptions and academic difficulties (Yewchuk, Delaney, Cunningham, & Pool, 1992). Chronic stress caused internally by perfectionism or externally from a stressful environment can impair a student's short- and long-term memory (Jacobs & Nadel, 1985). It diminishes his ability to sort out what is important and what is not (Gazzaniga, 1988). Stressful environments can trigger chemical imbalances in the brain, and these imbalances can result in impulsive, aggressive behavior (Jensen, 1998). The typical school environment can be very stressful for the twice-exceptional child who is trying to deal with academic difficulties, frustration, peer rejection, and feelings of being different (Bender, Rosenkrans, & Crane, 1999; Luthar & Zigler, 1991; Pianta & Walsh, 1998).

Resiliency Factors

Students' abilities to cope with and overcome risk and adversity are known as resiliency factors (Dole, 2000). These factors act as protective buffers to shield the students from adversity (Garmezy, 1991; Werner & Smith, 2001). Research has identified external and internal protective buffers present in students with learning disabilities who made successful transitions. They found that students with personality characteristics that elicit positive responses from others and those with good communication skills were more successful (Werner & Smith, 2001). As students acquired the skills necessary to use their abilities, they learned to set realistic educational and vocational goals. The students' self-efficacy increases with positive school experience (Dole, 2000). The development of problem-solving and planning skills results in an increased internal locus of control (Dole,

2000; Werner & Smith, 2001). Challenging learning opportunities, flexible teachers, and relevant work increases students' resiliency (Trail, 2008).

Self-Actualization

A research study conducted by the author examined the unique characteristics and experiences of twice-exceptional learners to determine what they need in order to thrive (Trail, 2008). Qualitative case study research methodology identified five themes that influenced academic achievement and satisfaction with life in twice-exceptional learners. Below is a brief explanation of the identified themes. Each theme will be addressed in greater detail in subsequent chapters.

Theme 1: Cognitive Characteristics

Participants' cognitive development was "out of sync" with their physical, social, and emotional development. They had a significant verbal and performance discrepancy on the Weschler Intelligence Scale for Children (WISC-IV); their Verbal IQ scores were 35–48 points higher than the Performance IQ scores. Executive functioning deficits made it difficult for these students to plan, prioritize, and organize. High levels of creativity contributed to nonconformity and independent thinking. Participants had strengths in the global style of conceptualizing information and struggled with sequential thinking. They preferred unstructured problems and disliked the structure many teachers imposed.

Theme 2: Educational Experiences

Twice-exceptional learners continue to be at risk in an educational system that does not understand their unique characteristics or needs. These students need challenging learning opportunities to develop their potential, not one-size-fits-all approaches. In the author's study (Trail, 2008), a focus on fixing the students resulted in defiant behavior and poor grades. An encouraging approach helped them develop the compensatory skills necessary to be successful. Participants were motivated when solving novel problems rather than completing drill and practice worksheets. They preferred relevant work and became defiant when forced to complete assignments they considered busywork.

Theme 3: Interpersonal Relationships

Twice-exceptional learners cannot develop positive peer relationships unless they have an opportunity to bond with peers of similar ability. Positive relationships with peers, teachers, and parents were essential for the social and emotional development of the twice-exceptional students in my study. Poor social skills and an anti-intellectual climate in school resulted in the bullying of one participant. Many of the others had good relationships with flexible teachers while inflexible teachers considered them to be "difficult students." Participation in extracurricular school activities extended learning opportunities and promoted affiliations with peers who had similar interests.

Theme 4: Intrapersonal Understanding

Dealing with both exceptionalities can be confusing and frustrating. Participants in the study exhibited intense emotions, anxiety, oversensitivity, and low self-esteem. How students viewed their success directly related to their ability to derive satisfaction from that success. Dysfunctional perfectionism was a serious problem for one participant. Counseling from a therapist who understood the characteristics and needs of twice-exceptional students was important to help the students in the study deal with depression, anxiety, dysfunctional perfectionism, and thoughts of suicide.

Theme 5: Self-Actualization

Educational experiences, interpersonal relationships, and intrapersonal understanding directly related to resiliency and achievement. Resiliency increased with supportive interpersonal relationships, positive educational experiences, and intrapersonal understanding. With realistic goals, internal locus of control, and the knowledge that they could be successful, the twice-exceptional learners in the study became self-actualized.

Self-Actualization Continuum

The self-actualization continuum shown in Figure 5 illustrates how the relationship between innate cognitive abilities, educational experiences, interpersonal relationships, and intrapersonal understanding influences twice-exceptional learners' academic achievement and satisfaction with life. Theme 1 provides the foundation. Themes 2, 3, and 4 are equally important for self-actualization. Continuums reflect the positive and negative extremes in each of these categories. Positive factors promote resiliency and achievement, while negative factors increase risk factors and can result in underachievement. Theme 5, self-actualization, results when there are more positive than negative influences on achievement.

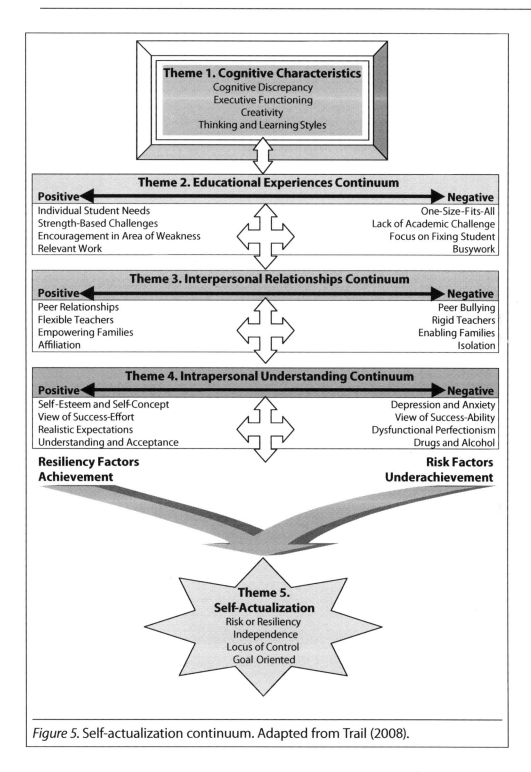

Figure 5. Self-actualization continuum. Adapted from Trail (2008).

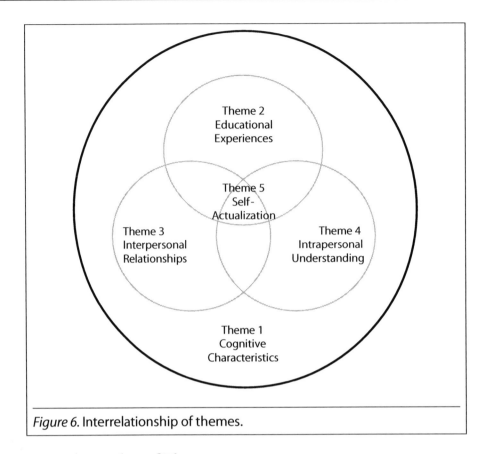

Figure 6. Interrelationship of themes.

Interrelationship of Themes

The interrelationship of the themes is illustrated in Figure 6. Cognitive characteristics are innate abilities that provide the foundation for educational experiences, interpersonal relationships, and intrapersonal understanding. Negative educational experiences, interpersonal relationships, and intrapersonal understanding diminish resiliency and achievement. Positive ones increase resiliency, achievement, and the likelihood of attainment of self-actualization.

Summary of the Implications of the Research Study on Self-Actualization

This research (Trail, 2008) revealed the following implications for the education of twice-exceptional learners.

First, twice-exceptional learners continue to be at risk in an educational system that does not understand their unique characteristics or educational needs. This research demonstrates the importance of providing challenging learning opportunities so twice-exceptional learners are able to develop their potential, which contributes to positive self-esteem and self-concept. Curriculum and instruction using a one-size-fits-all approach will not meet their needs. A flexible learning environment is important because it allows twice-exceptional learners to show what they know using their strengths and their preferred thinking and learning styles. These atypical learners need encouragement to develop the compensatory skills necessary to be successful. A focus on trying to fix twice-exceptional learners results in underachievement and defiant behavior. Finally, twice-exceptional learners need opportunities for relevant learning and creative expression, because this increases their motivation to learn.

Second, this research revealed the importance of interpersonal relationships for twice-exceptional learners. Positive interpersonal relationships with peers, teachers, and parents are essential for their social and emotional development. Twice-exceptional learners cannot develop positive peer relationships unless they have an opportunity to bond with peers who have similar interests and/or ability. This research exposed the negative consequences of peer bullying and an anti-intellectual environment. Positive relationships with supportive teachers directly influence the achievement of these twice-exceptional learners. They need empathetic teachers who will encourage them to develop the skills they need to be successful. Parents play an essential role in supporting and advocating for their children. Twice-exceptional learners need positive role models to help them realize they can be successful regardless of their disability. Participation in extracurricular school activities and community organizations extends learning opportunities and promotes affiliations with peers who have similar interests and/or abilities.

Third, intrapersonal awareness, understanding, and acceptance are essential for twice-exceptional learners because dealing with both exceptionalities can be very confusing and frustrating. Knowledge of their cognitive strengths, weaknesses, and preferred learning and thinking styles is important for the development of intrapersonal understanding. How students view their success directly relates to their ability to derive satisfaction from their success. One student could not accept his success because he viewed his giftedness as an "undeserved talent," something he was given that he did not earn. Another student recognized he had musical talent, and he learned he could grow that talent by investing effort. When he achieved success, he attributed it to effort and his self-esteem increased. Individual and family counseling provided by a therapist with specialized training related to gifted students may be necessary to help twice-exceptional students learn to deal with emotional issues.

Finally, this research revealed that educational experiences, interpersonal relationships, and intrapersonal understanding directly relate to resiliency and level of achievement. Resiliency increases with supportive interpersonal relationships, positive educational experiences, and intrapersonal understanding. Likewise, negative experiences and relationships increase the student's risk for underachievement, depression, and anxiety. Focusing on a realistic career goal gives twice-exceptional learners a reason for persisting through their frustration to achieve success. As twice-exceptional learners learn they can achieve their goals, they realize they can take control of their future. With realistic goals, internal locus of control, and the knowledge that they can be successful, twice-exceptional learners will become self-actualized.

Putting Research Into Practice

This research developed a complex, holistic understanding of twice-exceptional learners. It increases educators' understanding of how twice-exceptional learners' unique characteristics and experiences influence their level of academic achievement and satisfaction with life. Now the findings of this research will be used to guide educators through the process of identifying the needs of twice-exceptional learners and developing a comprehensive plan to meet those needs.

ASSESSMENTS

Advocates of twice-exceptional children have recognized the need for early identification and programming. Yet many twice-exceptional learners are not identified in elementary school because they manage to hide their disabilities. As these students progress into middle school, they experience extreme frustration trying to deal with both of their exceptionalities. The delay in recognition of their twice-exceptionality can result in social and emotional consequences that can be debilitating. Response to Intervention uses ongoing assessments to screen and monitor student progress, because students have diverse needs and their response to instruction and interventions are unique. The "well check" in health care used to screen and monitor infant development is a useful analogy for progress monitoring (Deno, 2009). It recognizes that an individual's rate of growth varies not only according to her ability, but instruction also influences growth.

Formative assessments are repeated frequently to monitor the student's performance. Information from the universal screenings and progress monitoring are useful in identifying students who are at risk of academic failure and students who are not making adequate progress. These assessments are quick and do not require extensive specialized training of teachers to administer. The assessment data documents student growth and is used to guide instruction and select interventions. Early intervention addresses the issues before the problems become more serious. The following are examples of the various types of assessments available to determine the students' current level of proficiency, identify areas of strength and weakness, and to monitor their progress toward achieving learning goals:

- *Universal Screening*: A quick assessment used to screen all students early in the school year to develop an initial baseline of students' acquisition of critical skills. It identifies students who are below or above expected performance criteria. The National Center on Response to Intervention (2009, 2010) reviewed these universal screening tools and found convincing evidence of their effectiveness:

- Discovery Education Assessment Predictive Benchmark: Group assessment in math and reading taking about 40 minutes to administer and score.
- Predictive Assessment of Reading (PAR): Individual assessment in reading taking 16 minutes to administer and score.
- System to Enhance Educational Performance (STEEP): Individual assessment of oral reading fluency taking 1 minute to administer and score.

- *Progress Monitoring*: Progress is assessed using repeated formative assessments at regular intervals throughout the school year to determine if students are making adequate progress, measure students' responses to intervention, and guide decision making. The National Center on Response to Intervention (2009, 2010) recommended the following tools for their effectiveness:
  - Curriculum Based Measurement in Reading (CBM-R): Measures letter sound fluency, maze fluency, passage reading fluency, and word identification fluency.
  - Monitoring Basic Skills Progress (MBSP): Monitors basic math computation and basic math concepts/applications.
  - Yearly ProgressPro: Measures math, reading language arts, and reading maze fluency.
  - Accelerated Math: Measures mastery of math skills.

Additional assessments may be necessary for students who are not achieving. The following assessment data can provide information on the students' general achievement, specific skill deficits, and cognitive processing problems. These norm-reference assessments compare the students' performances to a group of students on a normal distribution curve. These assessments can only be administered once a year.

- *Diagnostic Assessments*—Formal diagnostic assessments provide reliable in-depth information on students' acquisition of skills and can be used to select interventions that focus on specific skill deficits. These are examples of diagnostic assessments that can be used for reading or math:
  - Gates-MacGinitie Reading Tests (GMRT) Fourth Edition
  - KeyMath-3 Diagnostic Assessment
  - Stanford Diagnostic Reading Test (SDRT4) Fourth Edition
  - Early Reading Diagnostic Assessment (ERDA2) Second Edition

- Woodcock-Johnson III Diagnostic Reading Battery (WJIII-DRB)
- Woodcock-Johnson III Tests of Achievement (WJ-III)

- *Achievement Tests*—There are standardized tests used to measure skills and knowledge related to grade-level content standards. The tests are normed with children across the United States so parents and educators know where the student ranks when compared to other students. Results provide percentile rank, grade or age equivalent, standard score, and stanine. Some examples include:
  - Iowa Tests of Basic Skills (ITBS): Group-administered assessment of basic academic skills.
  - Woodcock-Johnson III Tests of Achievement (WJ-III): Individual assessment of oral expression, listening comprehension, written expression, basic reading skills, reading comprehension, reading fluency, math calculation skills, and math reasoning.
  - Weschler Individual Achievement, Second Edition (WIAT-II): Individual assessment of letter naming, phonological skills, pseudoword decoding, reading comprehension, spelling, written expression, numerical operations, math reasoning, listening comprehension, and oral expression.
  - Wide Range Achievement Test, Third Edition (WRAT-3): Measures development of reading, spelling, and arithmetic skills.
  - Stanford Achievement Test, 10th edition: Untimed assessment with flexible guidelines to measure students' progress toward achieving academic standards.
  - The Kaufman Test of Educational Achievement, Second Edition (KTEA-II): Individually administered test of math applications, reading decoding, spelling, reading comprehension, and math computation.

- *Cognitive Assessments*—Formal cognitive assessments are used to assess auditory processing, visual perception, processing speed, executive functioning, sequencing, memory, and attention. These tests are norm-referenced tests and although they cannot be used to monitor student progress, they can be used to gain valuable insights into students' cognitive strengths and weaknesses:
  - Cognitive Abilities Test (CogAT): Group-administered ability test battery to assess verbal, quantitative, and nonverbal reasoning and problem-solving skills.
  - Naglieri Nonverbal Ability Test (NNAT): Individually administered assessment of general reasoning ability.

- Wechsler Intelligence Scale for Children, Fourth Edition (WISC-IV): Individual assessment of cognitive strengths and weaknesses.
- Differential Ability Scales, Second Edition (DAS-II): Individual cognitive ability test that measures verbal and nonverbal reasoning.
- Kaufman Brief Intelligence Test, Second Edition (KBIT-2): Individually administered quick measure of verbal and nonverbal intelligence.

To gain a comprehensive view of the student's academic, social, and emotional development, use the following methods to collect additional information. As with other assessment data, use this information when developing a plan of intervention.

- *Functional Assessments*
  - *Behavioral*: A process used to identify the events that are causing and maintaining problem behaviors. It is useful in identifying antecedent events that trigger a problem behavior or increase its frequency. Information is used to develop interventions to teach acceptable alternative behaviors.
  - *Academic*: A process used to identify skill gaps and strategies that are not effective in order to develop interventions that will be more successful.

- *Additional Sources of Information*
  - *Observations*: Valuable information can be obtained through observing the student in the classroom and on the playground as he learns and interacts with teachers and peers.
  - *Interviews*: Parents, students, and teachers can provide an excellent source of information. Many twice-exceptional learners are very capable of discussing their instructional needs. Parents of these students can share valuable insights regarding the student's strengths, challenges, and interests. Do not underestimate the value of their contribution to the problem-solving process.
  - *Portfolios*: A portfolio is a collection of the students' work. Give students a folder in the classroom where they can put examples of their work. Educators, parents, and students can see a comprehensive view of students' growth.
  - *Checklists and Scales*: These can guide teachers and parents through a series of questions to gain specific information that can be used to inform instruction and interventions. The following scales and assessments can provide valuable information:
    - The Vineland Adaptive Behavior Scales, Second Edition (VABS-II): Measures an individual's personal and social skills

and adaptive behavior from birth to 90 years and includes survey interview and parent and teacher rating forms.

♦ Behavior Assessment System for Children, Second Edition (BASC-2): Evaluates the behaviors, thoughts, and emotions of children and adolescents.

♦ Gifted Rating Scales (GRS): Norm-referenced rating scale use to identify gifted and talented students.

Risk and Resiliency Continuum

The author's research (Trail, 2008) was used to develop the Risk and Resiliency Continuum in Figure 7. Each factor will either increase or decrease the student's resiliency. Simply circle the number that best represents the skill level of the student on each item. Items circled in the two lefthand columns are risk factors that can lead to underachievement. Factors in the two righthand columns contribute to the student's resiliency. Add up the scores in each column to determine if there are more risk or resiliency factors influencing the student's achievement.

DIVERSE NEEDS

Twice-exceptional learners have diverse cognitive, academic, social, and emotional needs that require a continuum of services. Review both qualitative and quantitative data to get a comprehensive view of the students' needs. In addition, gather samples of work and interview teachers, gifted and special education specialists, parents, and students. Analyze the data to identify the variables that are influencing the students' achievement and behavior. Use the assessment information during the decision-making process to guide instruction and selection of interventions. Decide if additional assessments are needed to get a comprehensive view of the students' cognitive, academic, social, and emotional needs.

Strengths and Challenges

Identifying the students' strengths and challenges will help the school team to identify inconsistencies in academic performance. Using the Strengths and Challenges checklist in Figure 8 will be helpful when selecting interventions to develop students' strengths and diminish the effects of their disabilities. Copy this form and ask every teacher who works with the student to complete the form. Each teacher will view the student differently depending on how well the student's strengths and learning style match the course content and their teaching style. In some subject areas, the student's gifted characteristics will be more

Risk and Resiliency Continuum						

Student: _____ **Grade:** _____ **Age:** _____

Teacher: _____ **Date:** _____

Cognitive Style						
Weakness ◄—————————————————————————————► **Strength**						
1	2	Verbal Ability	3	4
1	2	Nonverbal Reasoning	3	4
1	2	Visual Processing	3	4
1	2	Auditory Processing	3	4
1	2	Processing Speed	3	4
1	2	Memory/Attention	3	4
1	2	Creative Curiosity	3	4
1	2	Executive Functioning (Planning and Organization Skills)	3	4
Academic Achievement				
Weakness ◄—————————————————————————————► **Strength**				
1	2	Vocabulary and Communication Skills	3	4
1	2	Advanced Ideas and Opinions	3	4
1	2	Reading/Reading Fluency	3	4
1	2	Writing/Writing Fluency	3	4
1	2	Math/Math Fluency	3	4
1	2	Science	3	4
Interpersonal Relationships				
Weakness ◄—————————————————————————————► **Strength**				
1	2	Peer Relationships	3	4
1	2	Relationship With Teachers	3	4
1	2	Family Relationships	3	4
1	2	Relationship With a Caring Adult/Mentor	3	4
1	2	Affiliation in Clubs, Activities, or Organizations	3	4
1	2	Leadership Ability	3	4
Intrapersonal Understanding				
Weakness ◄—————————————————————————————► **Strength**				
1	2	Anxiety/Frustration/Depression	3	4
1	2	Personal Understanding	3	4
1	2	Personal Acceptance	3	4
1	2	Perfectionism	3	4
1	2	Realistic Expectations	3	4
1	2	Ability Success Effort	3	4
Self-Actualization				
Weakness ◄—————————————————————————————► **Strength**				
1	2	Locus of Control	3	4
1	2	Independence	3	4
1	2	Determination	3	4
1	2	Goal Attainment	3	4
+				+
	Risk or Resiliency			

Figure 7. Risk and Resiliency Continuum.

Strengths and Challenges (Page 1 of 2)		
Student: _____ **Grade:** _____ **Age:** _____		
Teacher: _____ **Date:** _____		
Directions: Read each statement with the student in mind. Then circle the number at the right that best represents the degree to which you disagree or agree that the statement is representative of the student.		
Gifted Potential (Chapter 4)		**Disagree-Agree**
• Advanced ideas and opinions		1 2 3 4 5
• Wide range of interests		1 2 3 4 5
• Sophisticated vocabulary		1 2 3 4 5
• Penetrating insights		1 2 3 4 5
• Superior verbal and communication skills		1 2 3 4 5
• Strong perceptual reasoning skills		1 2 3 4 5
• Advanced levels of reasoning and problem-solving abilities		1 2 3 4 5
• Highly creative, curious, and imaginative		1 2 3 4 5
• Specific talent or consuming interest in _____		1 2 3 4 5
Cognitive Style (Chapter 5)		**Disagree-Agree**
• Discrepancy between the WISC-IV Composite Index Scores		1 2 3 4 5
• Sequential thinker who learns step-by-step		1 2 3 4 5
• Conceptual thinker who comprehends the "big picture" and overlooks details		1 2 3 4 5
• Unable to think in a linear fashion		1 2 3 4 5
• Auditory learner who can easily remember verbal information		1 2 3 4 5
• Visual learner who needs to see it to process the information		1 2 3 4 5
• Difficulty following verbal instructions		1 2 3 4 5
• Slow processing speed, making it difficult to keep up		1 2 3 4 5
• Executive functioning deficits in planning, prioritizing, and organizing		1 2 3 4 5
• Problems with short-term memory; often forgetful		1 2 3 4 5
• Easily distracted and unable to sustain attention		1 2 3 4 5
• Sensory integration issues		1 2 3 4 5
Academic Achievement (Chapter 6)		**Disagree-Agree**
• Demonstrates inconsistent or uneven academic skills		1 2 3 4 5
• Difficulty expressing feelings or explaining ideas/concept		1 2 3 4 5
• Hates drill and practice assignments		1 2 3 4 5
• Avoids school tasks and often fails to complete assignments		1 2 3 4 5
• Poor penmanship and work can be extremely messy		1 2 3 4 5
• Problem completing paper-and-pencil tasks		1 2 3 4 5
• Appears apathetic, unmotivated, or lacks academic initiative		1 2 3 4 5
• Extremely frustrated by school		1 2 3 4 5
• Problems with fluency in ( ) writing, ( ) reading, and/or ( ) math		1 2 3 4 5
• Disruptive or clowning behaviors		1 2 3 4 5
• High energy level and needs to be actively engaged in learning		1 2 3 4 5

Figure 8. Strengths and Challenges checklist.

Strengths and Challenges (Page 2 of 2)	
Student: _____ **Grade:** _____ **Age:** _____	
Teacher: _____ **Date:** _____	

Interpersonal Relationships (Chapter 7)	Disagree-Agree
• Introvert who needs time to reflect and recharge	1 2 3 4 5
• Extrovert who is energized by being around others	1 2 3 4 5
• Poor social skills and demonstrates antisocial behaviors	1 2 3 4 5
• Difficulty with peer relationships	1 2 3 4 5
• Bullied by peers	1 2 3 4 5
• Relationships with family members are strained	1 2 3 4 5
• Capable of setting up situations to own advantage	1 2 3 4 5
• Withdrawn and has become increasingly isolated	1 2 3 4 5
• Affiliations with others through extracurricular activities or clubs	1 2 3 4 5
• Developing leadership skills	1 2 3 4 5

Intrapersonal Understanding (Chapter 8)	Disagree-Agree
• Highly sensitive to criticism	1 2 3 4 5
• Perfectionist and afraid to take risks on work or of making mistakes	1 2 3 4 5
• Easily frustrated and gives up quickly on tasks	1 2 3 4 5
• Blames others for mistakes and problems	1 2 3 4 5
• Relates success to "luck" and "ability"	1 2 3 4 5
• Believes success is achieved through hard work and effort	1 2 3 4 5
• Self-critical and has low self-esteem	1 2 3 4 5
• Experiences high levels of anxiety and depression	1 2 3 4 5
• Becomes easily frustrated	1 2 3 4 5
• Suffers from anxiety and/or depression	1 2 3 4 5
• High level of personal understanding and acceptance	1 2 3 4 5
• Holds reasonable expectations	1 2 3 4 5
• Can set realistic goals	1 2 3 4 5

Self-Actualization (Chapter 9)	Disagree-Agree
• Resilient	1 2 3 4 5
• Independent	1 2 3 4 5
• Internal locus of control, believes he or she is in control of destiny	1 2 3 4 5
• Focused and determined to attain goals	1 2 3 4 5

Additional Comments:

visible, in other subjects his or her disabilities will be more apparent, and some teachers will view him or her as average student.

The results of this checklist can lead to productive discussions between teachers with very different views of the same students. As teachers discuss these results they will learn about each student's learning preferences and gain insights into why a student is more successful in some classes. It is a good way to begin discussions of a student's strengths and challenges. Each heading on the chart refers to a corresponding chapter in this book that will provide additional information. Use this information during the problem-solving process as the team begins to define the learner's needs, develop goals, and select interventions. Reviewing each of the areas highlighted on the checklist will lead to the development of a comprehensive plan that will meet the diverse needs of each student. The goal is to reduce risk factors (challenges) and increase resiliency factors (strengths).

In order to meet the diverse needs of twice-exceptional learners, a K–12 continuum of services is required. In many instances these students are able to meet or exceed grade-level content standards and need additional challenge in order to experience a year's growth in subject areas related to their strengths. They learn at a faster pace and are able to conceptualize advanced ideas and concepts. Along with these strengths, they may have debilitating weaknesses that interfere with their academic achievement. Sometimes students will posses both strengths and weakness in the same academic area. For example, a student could be capable of solving complex mathematical problems, but struggle to learn multiplication facts or solve division problems following sequential steps. In addition, twice-exceptional students often have a number of social and emotional needs that must be addressed for these students to achieve optimum development.

The continuum of services for twice-exceptional learners must include articulated K–12 services to address cognitive, academic, social, and emotional needs. These students require services designed to nurture their potential, to deal with their deficits and promote academic achievement, to facilitate interpersonal relationships, and to foster intrapersonal understanding. The following is a brief summary of research supporting the importance of providing a continuum of services addressing students' needs in each area.

Nurture gifted potential. A key element in meeting the educational needs of twice-exceptional students is emphasis on developing strengths (Barton & Starnes, 1989; Baum, Emerick, Herman, & Dixon, 1989; Baum & Owen, 1988; Whitmore & Maker, 1985). Research has shown it is not good practice to focus on weaknesses at the expense of strengths; the result is poor self-esteem, lack of motivation, depression, and stress (Baum, 1984b; Whitmore & Maker, 1985). Chapter 5 is dedicated to nurturing the potential of twice-exceptional learners.

Support academic achievement. The gifted potential of twice-exceptional learners combines with learning challenges that negatively influence academic achievement. It is important to pinpoint deficit areas and provide explicit instruction relative to students' weaknesses (Barton & Starnes, 1989; Baum et al., 1989; Baum & Owen, 1988; Whitmore & Maker, 1985). Teachers should instruct students in compensatory strategies and provide accommodations while students are learning to compensate for their deficit areas. Chapter 6 focuses on strategies to promote academic achievement.

Foster interpersonal relationships. Twice-exceptional learners often find it difficult to develop meaningful interpersonal relationships. Positive interpersonal relationships provide the support students need in order to persist through difficult times. Encouraging teachers, accepting peers, empowering parents, and supportive mentors play an important role in increasing the resiliency of twice-exceptional learners (Trail, 2006). Learn more about interpersonal relationships and specific interventions in Chapter 7.

Promote intrapersonal understanding. Twice-exceptional learners have a difficult time dealing with their mixed abilities. Low self-esteem and dysfunctional perfectionism can have a negative influence on their achievement. It is crucially important for these students to understand and accept their strengths and challenges. Chapter 8 is packed with strategies to help twice-exceptional learners develop intrapersonal understanding.

CONTINUUM OF SERVICES

Twice-exceptional learners have diverse needs that require a continuum of services tailored to their individual needs. For many twice-exceptional learners the general education classroom can provide the appropriate modifications. Gifted and special education specialists can support the classroom teacher with specific interventions to provide students with additional challenge in their area(s) of strength and support in their area(s) of weakness. Some students will need small-group instruction to target specific areas of deficit and accelerated instruction in order to challenge them at an appropriate level. Other education specialists may provide interventions in the area of reading, writing, math, and/or speech. Students with behavioral, social, or emotional issues may need small-group or individual support from the school counselor, social worker, or school psychologist. Some students may require interventions at an intensive level. Radical acceleration, individual instruction, a school within a school, special schools, and dual enrollment are options for these students. Figure 9 summarizes a variety of interventions that should be included in a continuum of services for twice-exceptional learners.

Continuum of Service Delivery Options		
Universal Interventions	Classroom Instruction	• High-quality, research-based classroom instruction • Differentiated instruction that assesses students and adjust instruction accordingly to meet individual needs • Flexible grouping in classroom, grade level, or multigrade levels of students with similar abilities and/or interests for instruction • Most Difficult First allows students to demonstrate mastery of a concept and use time to study the topic in greater depth • Curriculum compacting involves assessing student knowledge and freeing up time for orbital or independent studies • Orbital studies are individual or small-group investigations revolving around a facet of the curriculum
Targeted Interventions	Gifted Education (Cluster or Small-Group Instruction/Intervention)	• Work with the classroom teacher to ensure the student is challenged at an appropriate level • Teach students critical thinking, creative thinking, and creative problem solving strategies • Provide instruction in time and project management • Coach students in setting long- and short-term goals
	Special Education (Cluster or Small-Group Instruction/Intervention)	• Assess students to determine skill deficits and provide explicit instruction • Work with the classroom teacher in meeting the learning needs of all students • Teach students compensatory strategies • Provide accommodations for struggling students
	Librarian	• Teach students research skills • Supervise research for independent study projects
	Specialists (Cluster or Small-Group Instruction/Intervention)	• Literacy specialists assist students with deficits in reading and writing • Occupational therapists assist students with sensory integration deficits and dysgraphia • Speech and language pathologists assist students with deficits in speech and language
	School Counselor and School Psychologists (Cluster or Small-Group Instruction/Intervention)	• Monitor students' social and emotional development • Supervise friendship groups and teach students relationship and social skills • Teach students coping and stress management strategies • Provide career and college planning
Intensive Interventions	Specialists (Individual Instruction/Intervention)	• Individualized instruction and counseling for students with intensive cognitive, academic, social, or emotional needs
	School Within a School	• A specialized school for gifted students, students with disabilities, twice-exceptional students, or other special group that resides within a regular school
	Acceleration and Dual Enrollment	• Acceleration opportunities that allow students to go to the next grade or level for instruction in a specific subject
	Magnet School	• Specialized schools for the arts or sciences that can be effective in meeting the needs of twice-exceptional learners
	Internships and Mentorships	• Opportunities for students to work with mentors and participate in internships to develop special talents.

Figure 9. Continuum of services delivery options.

Planning Continuum

Collaborative planning is necessary to develop a plan that will meet the diverse needs of twice-exceptional learners. The Twice-Exceptional Planning Continuum (see appendix) was created to guide educators through the problem-solving process. The next five chapters focus on each of the themes found to be essential for twice-exceptional learners to become self-actualized: Chapter 4 discusses how gifted potential can be nurtured, Chapter 5 provides strategies to support a student's cognitive style, Chapter 6 helps teachers encourage academic achievement, Chapter 7 provides assistance in fostering interpersonal relationships, and Chapter 8 discusses ways to promote interpersonal understanding. Chapter 9 discusses how to use the continuums in the appendix, and a detailed planning continuum is included in the appendix along with a sample continuum of interventions dedicated to each theme.

Summary

Twice-exceptional learners are at risk when their cognitive, academic, social, and emotional needs are not met. This chapter focuses on identifying student needs and providing a continuum of services to meet those needs. There are risk and resiliency factors that can influence a student's achievement in a positive or negative way. The Risk and Resiliency Continuum provided can identify those factors that put the student at risk and those that help the student develop resiliency. Review all of the qualitative and quantitative data to get a clear understanding of the student's abilities and disabilities. Use the data to define the student's strengths and challenges. Determine if additional assessments are needed to provide more specific information regarding the student's abilities. Use the information to develop a comprehensive plan with a continuum of services to meet the diverse needs of twice-exceptional learners. Develop measurable goals so the student's progress can be monitored and, based on the results, modify the plan until the student is achieving commensurate with her ability. The next five chapters will identify cognitive, academic, social, and emotional needs and provide specific strategies to address those needs.

Chapter 4

Nurturing Gifted Potential

A key element in meeting the educational needs of twice-exceptional students should be an emphasis on developing the students' strengths (Barton & Starnes, 1989; Baum et al., 1989; Baum & Owen, 1988; Whitmore & Maker, 1985). Unfortunately, twice-exceptional students often are excluded from gifted programming when they fail to meet general classroom expectations. Well-intentioned teachers tend to focus on the students' weaknesses in an effort to help them develop deficit skills. However, research has shown it is not good practice to focus on weaknesses because it can lead to poor self-esteem, lack of motivation, depression, and stress (Baum, 1984a, 1984b; Whitmore & Maker, 1985). This chapter will explore strategies to nurture the potential of twice-exceptional learners. Readers will gain a deeper understanding of programming elements that are critical for motivating students and developing their strengths. As twice-exceptional learners excel in their areas of strength, they develop the resiliency they need to persevere through the struggles of overcoming their disabilities.

SUPPORTIVE LEARNING COMMUNITY

Diversity and excellence are valued and celebrated in a supportive learning community. In such an environment, teachers recognize that students learn differently, and they are flexible in meeting the individual needs of their students. Instructional planning anticipates diverse learning needs and the unique characteristics of individual students. There is an appreciation for diverse and multiple perspectives. Teachers focus on the positive traits of their students because they know this builds confidence and resiliency. As teachers convey a belief in their students' abilities, it increases the students' achievement and improves their social and emotional status (Baum, Renzulli, & Hébert, 1995; Olenchak & Reis, 2002). Teachers should use a metacognitive approach so students gain a deeper knowledge of their strengths, weaknesses, and learning styles. Students should be encouraged to develop their strengths and supported in their efforts to improve deficit skills. Assessments must be ongoing and diagnostic, with the goal to provide instruction at a moderate level of challenge for optimum growth (Tomlinson, 1999). In a supportive learning community, students learn to set personal goals and support each other as they work to achieve their individual goals. Excellence is defined by individual growth and attainment of goals. Students believe they can be successful if they work hard.

Focusing attention on the development of strengths, intellectual capabilities, interests, and passions rather than disabilities is extremely important for twice-exceptional learners. When teachers encourage students to explore their interests, it excites their inner passions and motivates them to become achieving lifelong learners. Allowing students to use their preferred learning style for acquiring knowledge, processing information, and communicating what they have learned increases their success. As students experience success in their strength area, they become more confident in their abilities.

CHALLENGING CURRICULUM

All learners need instruction in their zone of proximal development (Vygotsky (1978). If the challenge level is too high, they will become frustrated. When the curriculum is not challenging enough, students can lose motivation and disengage from school. Greg, a twice-exceptional student told me,

> I just remember so much of school was just sitting and not doing anything except waiting for everyone else to catch up. That's basically what school is. If you finish early, you just sit and put your head down. I definitely spent a lot of time doing that. [During middle school] I started to

really feel it [school] was pointless, a waste of my time, and it made me angry that I had to deal with this obligation that I didn't care about.

It was difficult for Greg to maintain focus with a slow pace and repetitive instruction. He often finished his work early and hated waiting for his classmates to catch up. Lack of consistent academic challenge caused Greg to view school as an obligation rather than a place of learning. Gifted students need curriculum that is challenging, appropriately paced, and relevant, with a focus on higher level thinking and problem solving. In order to meet the needs of gifted learners, the curriculum should:

- clearly focus on the essential understandings and skills of the discipline;
- provide clear expectations that challenge students to analyze, interpret, and evaluate major trends and issues;
- focus on the essential skills, understandings, and methodologies of disciplines that are utilized by practicing professionals;
- explore the multiple facets of topics, issues, and problems in greater depth and complexity;
- promote the use of cognitive and metacognitive thinking and invite reflection; and
- allow students to use their strengths and preferred learning style to process information and to demonstrate what they learned in creative, relevant ways.

DIFFERENTIATE FOR DIVERSE NEEDS

Differentiated instruction provides options to meet the needs of students with a wide range of abilities. Teachers can provide the challenge gifted students need to remain engaged in the learning process and the support students with disabilities need to be successful. However, students who consistently fail lose their motivation to learn. For learning to continue, students must believe that hard work is required and their efforts will be rewarded with success. Students learn best with moderate challenge (Vygotsky, 1978, 1987). Twice-exceptional learners need differentiated, explicit instruction to develop their strengths and increase the skills necessary to become competent in their deficit areas. More time must be invested in developing strengths than remediating deficits. Ongoing assessment is necessary to ensure instruction is at an appropriate level.

Increasingly teachers are faced with the overwhelming task of raising achievement scores in low-performing students. Greg scored in the advanced level on state assessments, so his teachers were not concerned with his progress. He was able to master new concepts with little practice and hated the "drill-and-kill" assignments he was forced to do even though he had mastered the concepts. Greg complained that teachers did not care about what he learned; it was all about getting the busywork assignments in on time. At some point Greg remembers, "My achievement diverged from being the little kid getting perfect scores on everything to feeling like school was pointless, a waste of time."

The problem with school, according to Greg, is "It is never fast enough. I have spent so much time having to hear about things I already know. It's bad because I probably tune out things that I should know because I am not paying attention." He complained about being bored in school. Greg enjoyed the computer math class because he was able to progress at his own rate. He believes it is important to tailor programs according to individual needs. Greg continued, "I feel like if someone would give me a series of books and say you need to learn these concepts by this date in time and then you are going to take a test, I probably could have learned so much of what I have learned in a third of the time."

Ongoing Assessment

Assessment should be ongoing and diagnostic with the goal of helping individual students to increase their competency. The focus of assessment is on personal growth and self-reflection instead of the right answers. Use the information from assessments to:

- *Get to Know Students*—A variety of assessments can be used at the beginning of the school year to determine a student's strengths, interests, weakness, and preferred learning style.
- *Guiding Instruction*—Preassess before the unit begins to find out what students already know. If students need additional challenge, implement curriculum compacting and learning contracts to ensure students are challenged at a moderate level.
- *Assessing Progress*—Use assessment information to assist students in setting personal goals and charting their own growth. Continue to assess student progress throughout the unit to determine if they are making adequate progress, understand concepts, require explicit instruction to continue progress, or need additional challenge.
- *Evaluate Instruction*—End-of-unit assessments determine if the students have made adequate progress and successfully acquired the expected knowledge and skills.

Teachers can differentiate the content, process, and product according to students' readiness, interests, and learning profile in order to promote optimum growth (Tomlinson, 1999). Case studies found that differentiating the curriculum for gifted students had a negative impact on gifted students with learning disabilities. There was an increase in anxiety and depression until differentiation strategies were adjusted for the unique needs of these students; then the studies found substantial improvements in students' academic, social, and emotional status (Olenchak & Reis, 2002).

Curriculum and instruction should contain provisions that will enable students to progress through the content at an appropriate pace. It is recommended that teachers pretest before beginning instruction to find out what the students already know so they can plan instruction. The goal is to challenge students at an appropriate level and to reduce unnecessary drill and practice. The following are research-based interventions:

- *Flexible Grouping* matches students who have the same level of readiness, interest, or learning style. Interest surveys, learning profile inventories, exit cards, quick writes, and observations provide valuable information for grouping students. It is important for teachers to provide opportunities for students to work within a variety of groups to avoid turning groups into tracking. Groupings should be purposeful and geared to accomplish a curricular goal.
- *Most Difficult First* allows student to demonstrate mastery of a concept by completing the most difficult problems with 85% accuracy. This eliminates unnecessary drill and practice. Students can use the time to become a residential expert or work on an independent project.
- *Curriculum Compacting* is a process that determines what students already know and what they need to learn. It allows students who have demonstrated mastery or can master it quicker to buy time to study more challenging curricula or areas of interest (Renzulli & Reis, 1985). Students can use the time to learn more about a particular topic the class is studying or a personal passion area.

Content

The first thing to consider when developing a unit of study is the content you want your students to learn and understand at the end of the unit. A focus on the essential understandings and skills used by practicing professionals engages students in learning that is meaningful and relevant. Continuous progression in difficulty of content and skills is needed to keep twice-exceptional students engaged in learning. The pace of instruction should be tailored to individual needs. The more superficial spiral approach to learning focuses on developing automaticity through drill and practice and does not engage students in exploring the complexities of the content (Rogers, 2007). Learning isolated facts can be difficult for twice-exceptional students who are conceptual/holistic learners. On the other hand, when instruction focuses on broad-based issues, themes, or problems, this creates a framework or overview of new material, which helps students to conceptualize and process the information. This conceptual framework enables students to make connections within the discipline and across content areas, which are necessary for interdisciplinary problem-based inquiry and lead to greater understanding of complex issues (VanTassel-Baska, Bass, Ries, Poland, & Avery, 1998).

Process

The process refers to the tasks and assignments that help students make sense of the content. The complexity of the task must match the students' level of understanding. It is important to differentiate the process according to the students' readiness, interests, and learning style. Research showed gifted learners tend to prefer independent study and self-paced materials (Rogers, 2002). Effective teachers for twice-exceptional learners facilitate learning rather than dispense knowledge. They encourage students to become more independent, self-reliant learners. Providing options allow students to use their strengths and preferred learning styles to process information in relevant ways. Drill-and-kill assignments are replaced by assignments that engage the students in conceptual discussions, higher order thinking, problem-solving activities, and investigations of real-world issues.

Product

The product is the vehicle the student uses to demonstrate and extend what she has learned. It should cause students to rethink, apply, and expand key concepts and principles. Twice-exceptional learners need multioption assignments that allow them to use their strengths to demonstrate what they have learned. When assignments are open-ended, students need rubrics that set clear standards of high expectations. Finally, twice-exceptional learners must be coached and mentored to create authentic products and develop their potential.

Differentiating Content, Process, and Product

When differentiating instruction to meet the needs of gifted and twice-exceptional learners, follow these guidelines:

- Content:
    - Focus on broad issues, themes, or problems versus merely covering the required content. Use a multidisciplinary approach whenever possible so students can make connections across content areas.
    - Engage students in learning that is meaningful and relevant by exploring multiple perspectives and discussing current issues. Teach students the skills used by practicing professional.
    - Pretest to find out what the students know and eliminate unnecessary drill and practice. Utilize multiple texts, videos, Internet sites,

and supplemental resources to accommodate a students' interests, level of readiness, and learning profile.
- Implement flexible grouping within the classroom or across grade levels for instruction so students have an opportunity to explore topics with students who have similar interests, learning styles, or abilities.
- Allow the students to study a topic of interest in greater depth and complexity. They can become the classroom expert on the topic and share what they have learned with the rest of the class.

- Process:
  - Allow students to process the information they have learned in a way that is meaningful for them. Gifted students prefer to apply what they have learned to solve real problems.
  - Encourage students to develop independent learning skills.
  - Match the complexity of the task with the students' level of understanding and provide respectful, engaging, high-level tasks for all learners.
  - Provide daily challenges with a continuous progression of difficulty and provisions for students to progress through curricula at a pace appropriate for the individual.
  - Make learning relevant by teaching students the skills of the practicing professional such as investigation and research skills.
  - Support student learning with graphic organizers to help students understand concepts, guide note taking, process information, plan projects, and guide progress.
  - If the student is struggling, find out where the breakdown is occurring and provide explicit instruction. Utilize technology to assist students and increase their productivity. Support and encourage students to persevere through their frustration.

- Product:
  - Allow choice of topics and assignments so students can use their strengths and preferred style of thinking to demonstrate what they have learned.
  - Encourage self-evaluation of progress and final product by developing criteria and rubrics to accommodate a range of learners.

Differentiation Strategies

The following are some common differentiation strategies teachers can implement:
- *Flexible Grouping*: Students can be grouped for instruction and activities

to process information according to interests, learning styles, or abilities. The key is to group and regroup students often.

- *Compacting*: Assess students before beginning instruction to determine what they already know. Students who demonstrate mastery of content can work on an orbital, independent, or group project.
- *Most Difficult First*: If the students can complete a designated number of the most difficult problems with 85% accuracy, they have demonstrated mastery of the concept and do not have to complete the rest of the assignment.
- *Tiered Instruction and Assignments*: Different levels of instruction and/or assignments are designed for students with varying levels of proficiency.
- *Centers and Choice Boards*: Students are given a choice in activities or assignments. This allows students to use the strengths or preferred learning styles to process information or demonstrate what they have learned.
- *Think-Pair-Share*: Ask students to think about a problem or question, then share and discuss their ideas with another student. Finally, as a pair, the students share their insights with the class.
- *Zigsaw*: Students are grouped together to research a topic or problem. Each group then shares its expertise with the class.
- *Agendas*: Students have personalized agenda of activities they must complete.
- *Orbital Study*: Students select a facet of the curriculum to study in greater depth and become the classroom expert.
- *Independent Study*: Students design a project to investigate a topic of interest and complete the project under the supervision of their teacher.

EMPHASIZE HIGHER ORDER THINKING

Twice-exceptional learners need opportunities to develop their higher order thinking and problem-solving abilities. They need to be able to identify problems related to a particular area of study, create alternative solutions for the problem, select a viable solution, develop an implementation plan, and be able to communicate the solution to others. In order to do this they need to develop skills in critical and creative thinking. These skills are increasingly important in an information age where the knowledge base is growing at a phenomenal rate. Students will need to develop critical and creative thinking skills to be able to analyze, prioritize, problem solve, and create new knowledge.

Critical Thinking

Critical thinking involves logical thinking and reasoning. When students are critical thinkers, they consider the evidence and use relevant criteria to make decisions. It is a thoughtful way to interpret data that requires knowledge of logical inquiry and reasoning skills to appraise evidence, evaluate arguments, and draw conclusions. Critical thinking is the key defining characteristic in professional fields and academic disciplines. For students to be critical thinkers, they must consider the evidence and use relevant criteria to make decisions.

Teach students to be critical thinkers with activities that require them to:

- *analyze and classify*: separate or subdivide the whole into parts according to its qualities or characteristics;
- *compare and contrast*: determine the similarities and differences;
- *synthesize*: combine ideas to create something new;
- *transformation*: see new relationships; and
- *judge, evaluate, or critique*: determine the appropriateness of the information or solution.

Socratic questioning can also be used to develop students' critical thinking skills. Teachers pose questions in Socratic questioning to help students learn to think critically. The teacher professes ignorance and engages students in a dialogue of thoughtful, logical examination of topics in an effort to recognize contradictions and determine the validity of their ideas. Questions that focus on the process of thinking help students learn to think critically. This technique fosters student reflection by asking questions that stimulate thinking essential to constructing knowledge.

Creative Thinking

School curricula may not be honoring achievement represented by applications of knowledge and creative production. Teachers consistently identified general compliance and teacher-pleasing behaviors as success factors, skills, or behaviors used as important descriptors for students nominated for gifted programs (Kauffman, 1993). The negative connotations of giftedness and creativity may be misinterpreted as signs of problem behaviors (Reid & McGuire, 1995). Vaidya (1993) advocated using creativity tests such as the Torrance Tests of Creative Thinking to measure divergent thinking skills of fluency, flexibility, originality, and elaboration in order to determine the nature of the students' thinking, their individual needs, and diverse learning styles. Interventions for twice-exceptional students should encourage creativity, and instructional programs should focus on talent development. Thematic units, small-group instruction to promote discussions, curriculum compacting, research teams, and self-directed study are effective techniques for teaching creative thinking (Reid & McGuire, 1995).

Creative thinking and the process of creating something new stimulates students' curiosity and divergent thought. Provide opportunities for students to develop the following skills:

- *fluency*: producing many different ideas or solutions to a problem,
- *flexibility*: viewing a problem or idea from multiple perspectives and pursue new avenues of thought,
- *originality*: developing uncommon yet acceptable ideas or solutions, and
- *elaboration*: embellishing an idea or adding details to the thought process.

Brainstorming. Brainstorming activities encourage students to generate as many ideas as possible in a designated amount of time. All of the ideas are written down, and nobody is allowed to pass judgment on any of the ideas during the brainstorming process. Students may hitchhike, or add to, the ideas of another student. This process teaches students to be open-minded and increases their tolerance of others' ideas.

Creative Problem Solving. The Creative Problem Solving (CPS) process guides students as they solve problems in creative ways. Alex Osborn, cofounder of a successful advertising agency, coined the technique of brainstorming and the CPS model. Sidney Parnes continued Osborn's work teaching creativity workshops and courses (Davis, 1998). The process has a divergent thinking phase where students are asked to generate lots of ideas and a convergent phase where they focus on the best ideas and solutions. As students strive to understand a problem, define it, develop alternative solutions, and finally develop a plan of implementation for the best solution, they move back and forth between left and right hemispheric thinking (McCarthy, 1980; Torrance, 1981).

The CPS process utilizes creative and critical thinking to solve a problem. It involves the following steps, in this order:

1. *Fact Finding*: Gather facts concerning every known aspect of the problem to order to determine the who, what, when, where, why, and how.
2. *Problem Finding*: Clarify the problem and identify the real issues you need to focus in order to solve the problem.
3. *Idea Finding*: Brainstorm all of the possible solutions to the problem.
4. *Solution Finding*: Create criteria for evaluating the possible solutions to determine the best solution for solving the problem.
5. *Acceptance Finding*: Develop a plan for solving the problem and convince others the plan is the best possible solution.

More Higher Order Thinking

Another way teachers can have their students participate in higher order thinking is to emphasize the scientific method, a process of answering scientific questions through observation or by designing an experiment. Scientists use this method for determining cause and effect relationships. As students complete the steps in the scientific method listed below, they will use higher lever thinking:

1. *Define the Question*: Identify a question that defines what the research is designed to answer.
2. *Gather Information*: Use multiple sources to learn as much as possible about the problem.
3. *Hypothesis*: After researching the topic, determine the most likely outcome for the research.
4. *Experiment*: Develop and document a sequential plan for performing the experiment.
5. *Analyze Data and Draw Conclusions*: Analyze the data to determine if the hypothesis was true, false, or partially true.
6. *Communicate Results*: Communicate the process and results to others.

RESPECTFUL TASKS/RELEVANT WORK

Twice-exceptional learners frequently comment that school lacks real-world relevance. They complain that teachers do not care about what they learn, just about the work being turned in on time. Rather than the superficial spiraling approach that focuses on automaticity through drill and practice, gifted students benefit from experiential learning using inquiry and problem-based strategies (Rogers, 2007). Besides keeping twice-exceptional learners engaged in school, challenging curriculum is necessary to develop relevant knowledge, skills, and habits of mind, just as a practicing professional would. Research has demonstrated that when educators emphasize mastering the skills of practicing scientists, twice-exceptional students excel (Baum, Cooper, & Neu, 2001). For example, Greg's demeanor changed when he talked about an internship where he had an opportunity to work with leading scientific researchers. He told me he learned more in his internship than in all of the biology classes he had taken.

Twice-exceptional learners are motivated by assignments that challenge their higher level thinking skills and are bored by drill and practice activities. For example, Greg complained about the lack of challenging activities in his school, stating:

> I don't feel like I get that much out of school because I don't really pay attention to it. If it is relevant or interesting, I will pay attention. I'm sure people would look at my grades and say, "Obviously it is challenging, look at your grades." All of my bad grades come from classes that were a bunch of busywork in my mind and I don't do busywork. [For instance,] posters, I can't stand posters. I took an F in a class I had an A in this semester because I wasn't going to do the stupid poster. That is middle school stuff and I'm done with Elmer's glue and construction paper. I'm not doing it anymore. I'm sick of school. It's sad to me because I've come

to hate school so much, even my favorite subject. I don't know if I am going to do it any more.

Twice-exceptional students need to experience continuous challenge that escalates consistently as they develop understanding. Assignments ought to help students rethink, use, and extend what they have learned. They should be engaging, worthwhile, rigorous, and authentic, and should require students to employ methods and procedure used by professionals in the field. Twice-exceptional learners need opportunities to explore different perspectives; analyze and interpret problems/issues; synthesize theories, ideas, and themes; and finally, evaluate trends and issues.

Emphasis on developing each student's potential is a key element in meeting the educational needs of twice-exceptional students (Barton & Starnes, 1989; Baum et al., 1989; Baum & Owen, 1988; Whitmore & Maker, 1985). Greg needed opportunities to use his advanced knowledge, abstract thinking, creativity, and reasoning skills in discussions, challenging projects, and real-world assignments. Challenging learning opportunities in his strength area would help to prevent the stress that results when there is inadequate academic challenge. Teachers can play an essential role in mentoring the development of gifted potential by providing consistent challenge and opportunities for students to reflect on their progress (Rogers, 2007).

Teachers should include twice-exceptional learners in the planning process because it is important to give them a voice in their education. Like Greg, many twice-exceptional learners have a good understanding of what they need. For example, curriculum compacting would condense the course content and allow Greg to use this time to study a topic of interest in greater depth and complexity.

INDEPENDENT/SMALL-GROUP PROJECTS

Independent and small-group investigations allow students to explore their passions and interest areas. They build intrinsic motivation, provide opportunities to transfer knowledge to an authentic context, and foster the development of lifelong learning skills. Students can use their preferred style of learning to acquire, process, and communicate information. A skilled teacher or mentor is needed to teach students the skills they need to complete the investigation, to assist them in utilizing community resources, and to coach students through the process. As students explore different perspectives and develop essential understandings, they develop the habits of mind of practicing professionals. In order to accomplish this, students must learn the skills necessary to identify a question or issue, research a topic with primary and secondary resources, analyze and interpret the information, draw conclusions, make recommendations, and report their findings. To further challenge students, teachers can add a component for conducting research by following the steps of CPS or the scientific method.

Twice-exceptional learners will sometimes lack the executive functioning skills needed to plan, organize, or complete an independent research project. Students must be coached through the process the first time. Graphic organizers are helpful tools to guide students through this process. The Independent Research Project Plan of Study in Figure 10 outlines the step-by-step the procedure for developing a project proposal and timeline. As students complete each step, they enter the date it was completed and the teacher initials the form to document completion. By documenting each step, it is easy for both the teacher and individual students to keep track of their progress.

The teacher's role is to monitor the students' progress, provide encouragement, and coach students when they run into problems. However, it is important for students to learn to evaluate their own work. The Rubric for Independent Research Projects in Figure 11 provides a rubric students can use to evaluate their project. The teacher should go over the rubric with the students to help them gain a realistic view of their work.

SUMMARY

This chapter has focused on the importance of nurturing the potential of twice-exceptional learners. Well-intentioned teachers may focus on students' weaknesses, but this can result in anxiety, depression, and underachievement. In order for twice-exceptional learners to develop their potential, the learning environment must value individual differences with emphasis on the development of students' strengths and interests. Instructional planning should anticipate the diverse learning needs, characteristics, and learning styles of individual students. When teachers focus on thematic units and broad-based issues, it creates a conceptual framework for students to make connections across disciplines. Teachers should utilize differentiated instruction to meet the individual learning needs of students, pretest to find out what students know, use flexible grouping of students so the pace of instruction is appropriate for the individual, and provide for continuous progression through the curriculum. Learning should be relevant for students with teachers providing connections to real-world problems and issues. Teachers should assist students in developing the habits of mind and skills of practicing professionals by emphasizing higher level abstract thinking and problem solving. Assignments should involve respectful tasks and relevant work with choices for products so students can use their strengths and preferred learning styles to demonstrate what they have learned. As students complete independent and small-group investigations, they develop the advanced skills necessary to develop their potential.

	Estimated Time	Target Date	Date Completed
Date Due:			
Name(s):			
Step 1: Problem Statement: Identify a problem you want to investigate. State the problem using one or two sentences to explain what you are going to study and why it is important.			
Step 2: Purpose: Explain what you expect to accomplish as a result of this study.			
Step 3: Research Questions: Develop questions that reflect what you will answer in order to solve the problem you have identified.			
Step 4: Research: Use a variety of resources to gather information on your research topic. Sources should including a variety of books, articles, and web searches. Interviews, observations, and scientific experiments may also be used. Keep track of your resources and provide a listing in your references.			
Step 5: Synthesis: Summarize findings and make recommendations.			
Step 6: Sharing the Project: Share the key findings, discuss the implications, and make recommendations based on your research to an audience of your choice.			
Step 8: Evaluating the Project: Use a rubric to evaluate your independent study investigation and make recommendations for future investigations.			
Step 9: Reflection: Reflect on the positive and negative aspects of the investigation process. What will you do differently next time?			
Student's Signature: **Teacher's Signature:**			

Figure 10. Independent Research Project Plan of Study.

Self-Assessment Rubric for Independent Research Projects

Name: _____   Project: _____

	One Point	Two Points	Three Points
Use of Time	• I did not always use my time wisely. I became distracted and lost my focus.	• Most of the time I used my time wisely. I tried to stay focused, but at times I was distracted and did not progress as fast as I should.	• I developed a timeline, met at frequent intervals with my teacher, and completed each step by the designated due date.
Problem Statement	• My problem was too broad and needed to be more specific.	• My problem statement was adequate but it could be improved.	• My problem statement was well defined and articulated.
Purpose of Study	• The purpose of my study was not well defined.	• The purpose of my study was not specific enough.	• The purpose of my study defined my study.
Research Question	• My research question was vague and incomplete.	• My research question was clear but too broad.	• My research question was clear and well focused.
Planning	• My research plan needed to be more detailed and focused.	• My research plan needed to be more specific to guide my investigation.	• My research plan focused on a clear problem. I answered my research question.
Timeline	• I developed a timeline for my research project. However, my timeline was unrealistic and I was unable to meet the due dates.	• I was not able to meet all of the deadlines. I met with my teacher to develop an alternative plan.	• I completed the steps in my timeline by the due dates. I met with my teacher each week to keep him or her informed.
Research	• I could find only limited resources related to my problem.	• I found multiple resources but my investigation and research notes were not well organized.	• I used a variety of resources and conducted an organized investigation exploring multiple perspectives. I documented my resources.
Synthesis	• My project did not completely answer my research question.	• My project answered the research question and reflects my learning, but lacks detail and demonstrates limited understanding.	• My project answered the research question accurately and demonstrated a complex understanding of the topic.
Sharing	• My final project lacked organization and depth of knowledge.	• I shared the results of my research project but my presentation was not well organized.	• My presentation was well organized and presented to an appropriate audience.

Figure 11. Self-Assessment Rubric for Independent Research Projects.

Chapter 5

SUPPORTING COGNITIVE STYLE

Individual differences in the way twice-exceptional students think and learn can account for differences in individual performance beyond ability. Cognitive styles account for individual differences in the way these students process information in terms of cognition (Sternberg, Grigorenko, & Zhang, 2008). Failure to achieve academically may result from a mismatch between the students' cognitive style and the teacher's instructional style. Successful people learn to recognize their strengths and weaknesses. They are able to capitalize on their strengths and find ways to compensate for their weaknesses. Likewise, students will be more successful in school if they are aware of their strengths and weaknesses. If students can use their preferred style to process the information and to demonstrate what they have learned, the product or assessment will be a more valid representation of their level of knowledge. When students are able to use their preferred style to process information, they can use their strengths to demonstrate their knowledge. This chapter seeks to clarify cognitive processing as it relates to twice-exceptional learners by focusing on the most important cognitive dimensions and related deficits. Strategies are included to assist students to become more efficient learners and processors of information.

DIMENSIONS OF COGNITIVE STYLE

The way students organize and process information has a physiological basis that influences the approach they use when thinking, learning, organizing, processing, and representing information. Many suggestions have been posited that the two hemispheres of the brain function differently. The left hemisphere is credited with analytical reasoning and sequential processing of information. It specializes in language acquisition and arithmetic operations. The right hemisphere is more random and intuitive. It processes emotional, nonverbal, and spatial information in a nonlinear, holistic style. However, the whole concept of right-brain or left-brain thinking is too simplistic. In actuality, each hemisphere of the brain performs a variety of functions (Goldberg, 2001) and most tasks rely on both hemispheres. For example, speech is centered in the left hemisphere, but language functions occur in both hemispheres. The cerebral hemispheres of the brain are different structurally, biochemically, and functionally.

The hemispheres are connected by the corpus callosum, a tight bundle of nerve cells through which the left and right brain communicate with each other. Researchers are learning more about the role each hemisphere plays in learning. Of particular interest to researchers is how the hemispheres communicate with each other. Recent findings indicate the right brain processes novel situations and the left brain processes routine information. With sufficient repetitions, the novel information shifts from the right to the left brain, becoming routine. The time required for this transition varies from person to person (Sousa, 2003). When there is a breakdown in the communication between the two hemispheres, it is difficult for skills to become fluid and automatic. This problem affects fluency in reading, writing, and math computation in many twice-exceptional learners.

Students are more successful when the left and right hemispheres function in conjunction with one another. They are able to shift back and forth between hemispheres in response to the nature of the task. As a result, students with an integrative style of processing are more successful in school because they can utilize either style depending on the task's requirements. When one hemisphere is more dominant, students have weaknesses in some areas and strengths in others. Students with learning disabilities often encounter problems processing information.

Greg, like many twice-exceptional learners, had a conceptual style of processing information, which meant he tended to focus on the broad concepts and overlook details. He could solve math problems in his head and found it very tedious to write out the sequential steps. He preferred finding alternative ways of solving problems and hated doing them the way the book taught. He preferred unstructured problems and disliked the structure many teachers imposed (Sternberg & Zhang, 2001). Whole-to-part conceptual teaching that focused on concepts, principles, issues, and generalizations helps students to use their strengths in reasoning and critical thinking to solve scientific and mathematical problems (Rogers, 2007).

Just as students process information in different ways, they also have different styles of learning and thinking. The problem with learning styles is the sheer number of different theories, schemes, or models in existence. For example, Coffield, Moseley, Hall, and Ecclestone (2004) found 71 different schemes of learning styles in their review of the literature and indicated the existence of more. It can become very confusing and overwhelming for an educator trying to choose which best fits her students. Each of these models has its own unique approach, a specific assessment to identify individual styles, and recommendations for teachers. However, Pashler, McDaniel, Rohrer, and Bjork (2009) found only limited research on the validity of learning style assessments. They concluded there was a lack of credible evidence to justify the cost and time requirements to incorporate learning style assessments in general educational practice.

The whole idea of cognitive or learning styles can be confusing, but it is important to take into account individual differences when planning. An awareness of the different styles can help educators to develop learning environments that will meet the individual needs of a wider range of students. Sensitivity to individual learning differences when planning instruction and assessment improves student achievement (Sternberg & Zhang, 2001). Therefore, it is my recommendation that educators do their best to provide students with a variety of ways to access information, provide choice in the way students can apply and practice what they have learned, and allow students to demonstrate their knowledge using their preferred style. I think it is important to guide students in reflecting on the learning process so they will learn how to capitalize on their strengths and compensate for their areas of weaknesses. It is all about metacognition—learning about how you learn so you can not only become a consumer of knowledge, but a producer of knowledge by using what is learned to solve problems and construct new meanings.

The following sections on dimensions of cognition are my attempt to present the information on cognitive processing styles that influence the achievement of twice-exceptional learners in an easy-to-understand format. The dimensions represent opposing styles of processing information. Individual student preferences are located somewhere on the dimension. Students at the extreme ends have a stronger preference for that particular style. Students in the center of the dimension are more flexible and can use the style most suited to the task. When teachers provide choices in the way students access information, process knowledge, and demonstrate what they have learned, they allow students to learn using their preferred style. By providing choices, teachers can create the ideal learning situation where students can select options that combine their preferred way of learning with varied task requirements to create an optimum learning environment. Three dimensions are examined with suggested strategies for students with specific strengths and deficits in each dimension.

Auditory-Visual Dimension

The auditory-visual dimension is reflective of the students' preference to learn through an auditory or a visual style. Some students find they learn best when listening to lectures and that their understanding of the topic increases as they discuss issues. Their ability to retain the information increases when they use their verbal skills to process information. Other students learn and retain the information more efficiently when it is presented visually in a video, pictures, or graphic organizers. Students with a strong preference for visual learning often have deficits in auditory processing. Likewise, students with an extreme strength in auditory style of learning may experience difficulties interpreting charts and graphs.

Auditory learners prefer to learn through listening to lectures or discussions. They like to talk things through and share their viewpoint with others. Reading text aloud helps them to understand the information because until they hear the written information it may have little meaning. Auditory learners interpret underlying meanings through listening to tone of voice, pitch, and speed. They may have a difficult time with visual tasks such as recognizing letters, words, numbers, and spelling. Students with weaknesses in visual processing tend to ignore operation signs and have a difficult time checking work for accuracy. Visual tracking problems can reduce reading speed, leading to reading comprehension problems. Learning information presented visually on the board or through charts, graphs, or maps may be difficult. Students may inaccurately copy information, ignore mathematical operation signs, and transpose letters and numbers. Handwriting may be illegible because of an inability to stay within the lines and margins.

> The following strategies are effective for auditory learners and/or students with weaknesses in visual processing:
> - Provide adequate verbal explanations when information is presented visually in charts, graphs, and graphic organizers.
> - Encourage students to read the information out loud and use self-talk as they view visual images.
> - Use color overlays, guides, or three-finger tracking when reading to help students with visual tracking.
> - Have students turn the paper vertically when doing math calculations to help them keep numbers in line.

- Color code visual material such as operation signs on math papers so important information is more prominent.
- Provide preferential seating at the front of the classroom and periodic breaks to reduce eye fatigue.
- Decrease white space on paper so it is not overwhelming for students with weak visual processing.
- Provide the student with copies of information from overheads and the board.

Visual learners think in pictures and learn best when information is portrayed in pictures, charts, graphs, illustrated books, PowerPoint presentations, videos, and handouts. They prefer to sit in the front of the classroom so they can view the teacher's body language and facial expressions to gain a better understanding of the content of the lesson. Taking detailed notes during classroom lectures or discussions is helpful because seeing the information helps them to understand it. Some visual learners prefer to draw detailed diagrams, webs, or pictures instead of taking written notes. Visual learners may appear inattentive during lectures. They tend to misinterpret verbal instructions, find it difficult to remember verbal information, and are distracted by background noise. The inability to distinguish between fine differences in speech can result in mispronunciation and poor phonological awareness. A weakness in decoding skills leads to difficulties in reading and spelling. Short-term memory deficits result when the brain cannot hold information long enough for it to be processed.

The following strategies are effective for visual learners and/or students with weaknesses in auditory processing:

- Use adequate visual supports such as charts or graphs to support new learning and demonstrate relationships. Provide written outlines or graphic organizers for students to complete during lectures to help them focus on important information.
- Provide preferential seating where the student can see the teacher's face and will not be distracted by extraneous noise. Check frequently to make sure the student understands important information.
- Assist students in learning how to listen for important information and key words.
- Provide clues when presenting key information such as raising your voice or tapping the student's shoulder.
- Make verbal instructions concise and present them in short, simple sentences or paraphrase them. Encourage students to ask questions to clarify information.

- Have students highlight important information while reading to improve their comprehension and activate visual memory. Provide copies of reading material so students can highlight the important information as they read.
- Use a multisensory approach for students learning to read and to teach spelling rules.
- Provide frequent breaks so students with auditory processing deficits will not become fatigued.

Sequential-Conceptual Dimension

Some students learn best sequentially step-by-step, while others need to transform information to gain a conceptual understanding before they can understand the facts. Sequential learners tend to do better in school because most curriculums are developed sequentially in a step-by-step process. Conceptual learners cannot make sense of facts when they do not see the relationships. Learners at the extreme ends of this dimension have a strong preference for either sequential or conceptual styles of processing, whereas learners in the center of the continuum have less preference and can learn easily when information is processed sequentially or simultaneously (Riding, 1997).

School curriculums frequently break down information sequentially into component parts, and instruction focuses on each component. Information is compartmentalized and then specific aspects are studied. The compartmentalization of information can sometime become rigid. Although students who process information this way can readily memorize details and learn isolated facts, they can have a difficult time understanding the underlying concepts. Students with weaknesses in conceptual learning frequently achieve in elementary school, but later experience difficulties with reading comprehension, math reasoning, and creative writing. Reading difficulty can manifest as problems with general comprehension and understanding irony, inference, sarcasm, and humor. In math, students have problems solving story problems and generalizing to new situations. General understanding and global awareness are problems for students who focus more on the specifics.

The following strategies are for students with strengths in sequential processing and/or weaknesses in understanding conceptual concepts:
- Provide a conceptual overview when beginning a lesson and summarize at the end of the lesson to help students develop a conceptual understanding.
- Be sure to show students how facts fit together to build a conceptual understanding of the topic.

- Provide graphic organizers, charts, or outlines for use when taking notes during lectures so the students will be able visualize the "big picture."
- Encourage students to go beyond superficial understanding and actively seek a conceptual understanding.
- Show students how what they are learning relates to real-world situations.
- Ask students to summarize their reading assignments to see if they understand the underlying principles.

Conceptual thinkers focus on concepts, tend to overlook details, and have difficulty with sequential steps. Students may be able to solve math problems in their head, but find it very tedious and extremely difficult to write out the steps. These students prefer unstructured problems and dislike the structure many teachers impose (Sternberg & Zhang, 2001). Whole-to-part conceptual teaching focusing on concepts, principles, issues, and generalizations would allow these students to use their strength in reasoning and critical thinking to solve scientific and mathematical problems (Rogers, 2007). Actively searching for meaningful context to create a conceptual understanding helps these students to establish relationships between the parts to gain a conceptual understanding of the topic. Students with weaknesses in sequential processing can have learning difficulties in the area of basic reading, math computation, expressive language, and writing mechanics. Remembering detailed information such as names, dates, formulas, and steps can be tricky for these students. Deficits in sequencing can make it difficult to remember the sequential steps needed to form letters, thereby reducing handwriting speed and automaticity. It also can diminish reading speed and fluency as well as the student's ability to sound out words. These students can have trouble determining the sequence of a story or following step-by-step directions.

The following strategies are for students with strengths in conceptual understanding and/or weaknesses in sequential learning:

- Begin lessons with a conceptual overview of the topic or whole-to-part conceptual teaching with a focus on concepts, principles, issues, and generalizations.
- Provide a graphic organizer or outline to guide thinking and note taking during lectures and help students to see the connections between concepts.
- Help students who lack writing fluency and/or cannot remember spelling and grammar rules master keyboarding, word processing, and using spelling/grammar checkers.
- Encourage students to use mnemonics to help them remember formulas and steps.
- Make assignments open-ended to allow students to use their strengths to solve relevant problems.

Convergent-Divergent Dimension

Both convergent and divergent thinking are involved in creative problem solving and they complement each other. Research findings indicate teachers can improve student achievement by helping low achievers learn how to use both the left and right hemispheres of the brain to process information in conjunction with each other. McCarthy (1980) and Torrance (1981) suggested Creative Problem Solving, because this specific process provides repeated experiences in using both left and right hemisphere styles of learning and thinking. As students strive to understand a problem, define it, seek alternative solutions, develop a plan of implementation for the best solution, and evaluate the process and outcomes, they move back and forth between left and right hemispheric thinking. This increases the integration of the left and right hemisphere, improving higher order thinking and problem-solving skills.

Convergent thinking is the process of bringing together information from a variety of sources to solve a problem or produce the correct answer. Students strong in convergent thinking may be weak in divergent thinking. Students use convergent thinking in school when they complete multiple-choice tests. It is the converging of thinking and narrowing of options in order to choose the correct answer. In Creative Problem Solving, students use convergent thinking when defining the problem, selecting the best solution, and developing steps to implement the plan. Students with a weakness in divergent thinking have a difficult time brainstorming creative ideas and novel solutions. Their center of attention is on choosing the right answer rather than examining all of the possibilities. These students can focus on the specific homework assignment and not get distracted by all of the possibilities.

> The following strategies are for students with strengths in convergent thinking and/or weaknesses in divergent thinking:
>
> - Teach students the Creative Problem Solving process because when they use this process they are alternating between convergent and divergent thinking.
> - Use the technique of SCAMPER to help students generate more divergent ideas. SCAMPER stands for Substitute; Combine; Adapt; Modify, Magnify, or Minify; Put to other uses; Eliminate; and Reverse or Rearrange.
> - Utilize the technique of brainstorming whenever it is helpful for students to generate creative ideas for topics for a writing assignment or ideas for a project.
> - Pose the questions of who, what, where, when, why, and how to help students consider all aspects of the assignment or problem.

Divergent thinking is associated with creativity and out-of-the-box thinking. This type of thinking involves looking for unique, novel ideas. It involves fluency, flexibility, originality, and elaboration of ideas to develop unique solutions needed to solve complex problems. Typically, convergent rather than divergent thinking is emphasized in school and conformity is valued (Skrtic, 1992). This can set the stage for potential dissonance between gifted students and school. Conformity, commonality, and rigidity that are typical in schools are problematic for many gifted children (Reid & McGuire, 1995). School curriculums may not be honoring achievement represented by applications of knowledge and creative production. Divergent thinkers prefer applications of learning in real-life situations (Torrance & Ball, 1979). They are motivated by the challenge of solving novel problems (Beckley, 1998), generating unique ideas, and producing creative solutions (Whitmore & Maker, 1985). Students with strengths in divergent thinking may struggle with convergent thinking, such as having a difficult time selecting the correct answer on a multiple-choice test because they tend to think of all of the possibilities instead of eliminating choices.

> The following strategies are for students with strengths in divergent thinking and/or weaknesses in convergent thinking:
>
> - Teach students the Creative Problem Solving process because when they use this process they are alternating between convergent and divergent thinking.
> - Use the technique of SCAMPER to help students generate more divergent ideas.
> - Provide graphic organizers to help students organize their projects.
> - Teach students to create a to-do list and prioritize what needs to be accomplished.
> - Provide explicit instruction and different strategies to help students with organization and time management.
> - Give divergent thinkers the challenge of creating something new, planning activities, or designing projects. These students like to make their own rules and design their own structures.
> - Provide open-ended questions as these students have a difficult time answering multiple-choice or true/false tests.
> - Give students the organizer in Figure 12 to teach them how to summarize. Summarizing is difficult for students with weaknesses in convergent thinking.

COGNITIVE ASSESSMENTS

Twice-exceptional students' strengths can mask their disabilities. Conversely their disabilities can mask their strengths, creating a unique learner profile. Cognitive assessments can provide specific information on students' strengths and can be used to identify hidden disabilities. In an investigation of students

Summarize: A good summary begins by stating the main idea and then presents the important supporting details in a brief, concise manner.	
1.	Read the passage.
2.	Identify the main idea:
3.	Identify supporting details: a. b. c. d.
4.	Summarize the main idea and supporting details in your own words:

Figure 12. Graphic organizer for helping students summarize what they have read.

with superior IQ's who had learning disabilities, Schiff et al. (1981) reported a significant verbal-performance discrepancy on the Wechsler Intelligence Scale for Children–Revised (WISC-R). This is one of the most frequently used cognitive assessments that gives insight into a child's strengths and weaknesses. The students in this study had above-average verbal comprehension and expression skills along with numerous creative talents. The subtest scatter, or discrepancy between the subtest scores, was notably greater for twice-exceptional learners than those obtained for children with disabilities or for typical children (Schiff et al., 1981). Research on students of average intelligence with learning and reading disabilities found they scored consistently lower on the "ACID" subtests: Arithmetic, Coding, Information, and Digit Span (Kaufman, 1979). Students with disabilities, who had superior intelligence, scored lower on the subtests of Arithmetic, Coding, and Digit Span. They had much higher scores on the Information subtest (Schiff et al., 1981). Lower scores in processing speed resulted in short- and long-term memory retrieval problems when time pressures were in place.

Cognitive disabilities diminish the brain's ability to process information. Basic automatic skills such as graphomotor speed, perceptual scanning, sequencing, organization, and study skills are at the center of twice-exceptional students' difficulties (Barton & Starnes, 1989). Twice-exceptional students can experience problems with auditory memory (Fall & Nolan, 1993; Gerber, Ginsberg, & Reiff, 1992; Maker, 1982; McGreevey, 1992; Miner & Siegel, 1992; Waldron & Saphire, 1990; Whitmore, Maker, & Knott, 1985) and visual memory (Fall &

Nolan, 1993; Miner & Siegel, 1992; Whitmore & Maker, 1985; Williams, 1988); have attention deficit disorders; and display difficulty in following a sequence of verbal directions (Vaidya, 1993) and with executive functioning or speed of processing information (Trail, 2008).

Wechsler Intelligence Scale for Children-IV (WISC-IV)

I have included this section on the WISC-IV because it is one of the most frequently used cognitive assessments. This assessment can give insights related to students' cognitive strengths and weaknesses. However, it is important to remember that the Full Scale IQ (FSIQ) score is not a reliable indicator of ability if there is a discrepancy of 23 points or more between the Verbal Comprehension Index, Perceptual Reasoning Index, Working Memory Index, or Processing Speed Index. The Verbal Comprehension Index (VCI) and the Perceptual Reasoning Index (PRI) can be used as independent measures of ability in those specific areas.

The WISC-IV composite and subtest scores can be compared to the brief descriptions below to get a better understanding of the students' strengths and weaknesses. Use this information to guide the selection of specific interventions. The average score on the four indexes is 100, and the average score on the subtest is 10 with the highest score of 19 and the lowest score of 1. It is the discrepancies between the scores that account for inconsistent classroom performance. When reviewing test scores, it is important to look for high scores indicating areas of strength and low scores indicating areas of weakness. Use the information provided below (see Wechsler, 2003, for more information) to identify individual strengths and weaknesses that should be addressed in the Individualized Education Program (IEP).

- *Verbal Comprehension Index (VCI)* measures verbal conceptualization. It assesses the child's ability to listen to a question, develop a solution, and express the answer aloud. VCI taps preferences for verbal information, difficulty with the unexpected, and desire for more time to process information.
  - The *vocabulary* subtest measures word knowledge, language development, long-term memory, and verbal concept formation. Auditory perception, comprehension, conceptualization, abstract thinking, and verbal expression are employed. It includes questions concerning the meaning of words.
  - The *similarities* subtest is a measure of abstract, logical thinking and reasoning. It requires children to determine how two concepts are alike.
  - The *comprehension* subtest measures verbal reasoning, comprehension, conceptualization, and expression. Knowledge of conventional

standards of behavior, social judgment, maturity, and common sense are involved. It includes questions about social situations.

- The *information* subtest (supplemental, not included in index score) measures general cultural knowledge and ability to acquire, retain, and retrieve factual knowledge. It requires skills in auditory perception, comprehension, and verbal expression.

- The *word reasoning* subtest (supplemental, not included in index score) measures verbal comprehension, analogical and general reasoning, and the ability to integrate and synthesize information and generate alternative concepts. It requires trial-and-error learning as children are given one to three clues and asked to determine what is being described.

- *Perceptual Reasoning Index (PRI)* measures nonverbal and fluid reasoning. It assesses students' abilities to examine a problem using visual-spatial and visual-motor skills, organize their thoughts, and create and test solutions. PRI taps preference for visual information, comfort with novel unexpected situations, and preference to learn by doing.

  - The *block design* subtest measures ability to analyze and synthesize an abstract design and reproduce it. Visual perception, organization, visual-motor coordination, and simultaneous processing is involved. It is a timed test requiring children to recreate a block pattern design.

  - The *picture concepts* subtest measures fluid reasoning, perceptual organization, and categorization. Children are shown rows of pictures and asked to find the pictures that have a common bond.

  - The *matrix reasoning* subtest measures fluid intelligence. Children are shown a picture and asked to identify the missing part.

  - The *picture completion* subtest (supplemental, not included in index score) measures visual perception and organization, concentration, and visual recognition of details. It assesses students' abilities to recognize familiar items and identify the missing parts.

- *Working Memory Index* assesses the ability to memorize, hold information in short-term memory, concentrate, and manipulate information in higher order thinking. It is important in concentration, planning ability, cognitive flexibility, sequencing skills, and ability to self-monitor.

  - The *digit span* subtest is a measure of students' encoding, auditory short-term memory, auditory processing, sequencing skills, attention and concentration, and rote learning. Children are given sequences of numbers orally and asked to repeat them as heard or in reverse order.

  - The *letter-number sequencing* subtest involves sequencing, mental manipulation, attention, and short-term auditory memory. Children are given sequences of letters and numbers. They are asked to repeat the numbers in numerical order and the letters in alphabetical order

- The *arithmetic* subtest (supplemental, not included in index score) assesses abilities in mental manipulation, concentration and attention, short- and long-term memory, numerical reasoning, sequencing, and fluid logical reasoning. Children mentally solve orally presented arithmetic problems.

- *Processing Speed Index* assesses children's abilities to focus, scan, and sequentially order visual information. It requires visual perception, scanning, organization, and multiple motor responses. The tasks require executive control of attention and sustained effort. Decreased processing speed can impair the effectiveness of the working memory.
  - The *coding* subtest measures visual-motor dexterity, nonverbal short-term memory, speed, and accuracy. Children use a key to copy geometric symbols and shapes.
  - The *symbol search* subtest measures processing speed, short-term visual memory, visual-motor coordination, and visual discrimination. Children are given rows of symbols and they must identify the target symbols in each row.
  - The *cancellation* subtest (supplemental, not included in index score) measures processing speed, visual selective attention, and vigilance. Children mark lines through objects that do not belong in a page of randomly arranged objects.

Significant cognitive discrepancies are typical for twice-exceptional learners (Schiff et al., 1981). They can have superior verbal abilities and excellent communication skills that increase teachers' expectations for academic achievement. Teachers do not understand that the inconsistent academic performance of twice-exceptional students is a result of discrepancies in their cognitive functioning. Weaknesses in sequencing, short-term memory, fine-motor dexterity, processing speed, and perceptual organization have a negative influence on their achievement. Cognitive disabilities diminish the brain's ability to process information and cause problems with basic automatic skills such as graphomotor speed, sequencing, organization, and study skills (Barton & Starnes, 1989). Cognitive assessments provide valuable information when developing individual learning plans.

Sally was identified by Child Find when she was just 4 years old. Assessments showed she was 2 years ahead of her peers in some areas and 2 years behind in others. She struggled in her early elementary years because of problems with auditory processing. She had a difficult time understanding information presented verbally. Teachers frequently commented on her inability to follow verbal directions. Her reading decoding skills developed slowly and she mispronounced certain sounds. She learned many words by sight and could read words she knew. However, she was in second grade before she learned how to sound out words. Once she learned to combine the sounds and syllables to form words, she quickly became a proficient reader. Academic performance improved when she was able to read the directions. As she learned to take notes during lectures, she found that she could remember the information if she wrote it down. Her academic achievement steadily improved and she graduated sixth in her class.

Greg's parents reported that he obtained developmental milestones at a somewhat accelerated pace. For example, he spoke his first word at 7 months and began speaking in simple sentences at 12 months. He taught himself how to read when he was 4 years old and could remember the excitement he felt the moment he "realized the symbols meant something, that there was a message in there. I just remember a real sense of pride. One of my earliest memories was actually being able to read a little child's primer to my parents." Greg acknowledged his preschool and kindergarten years in a Montessori school as his best time in school: "I really liked how it was very flexible and they let you follow your interests."

For Todd, there were early indications of advanced development as he met developmental milestones early. He spoke his first words at 10 months and spoke in sentences at 1 year 6 months, using a large vocabulary. He recognized letters at 2 years 3 months, counted to 10 at the age of 3, and could tell time by age 4. Todd also learned to read prior to attending kindergarten. His physical milestones, though, lagged behind those of typical children. He struggled with physical coordination and walked at 1 year 3 months, but did not learn to tie his shoes until age 5.

The WISC-III Index Scores showed in Table 1 further demonstrate discrepancies for both Todd and Greg. Greg scored in the 99.6th percentile and Todd scored in the 99.9th percentile on the Verbal Comprehension Index Score, which is exceptionally high. Greg scored in the 3rd percentile on the Process Speed Index Score, which is exceptionally low, with only 3% of the students taking this test scoring lower. Slower processing speed results in short- and long-term memory retrieval problems when time pressures are in place. Todd scored slightly below average in the 47th percentile in Processing Speed and 63rd percentile in Perceptual Organization. These discrepancies can indicate learning disabilities, even when the lowest score is in the average range (Webb et al., 2005). Both students were identified as twice-exceptional by educational consultants, but neither student was identified for special education services by their school district.

Close examination of the scores presented in Table 1 reveals a significant scatter that also is typical of many twice-exceptional students (Webb et al., 2005). Todd's and Greg's scores for Information, Similarities, Arithmetic, Vocabulary, and Comprehension are in the superior range of 14 and above. It should be noted again that 19 is the highest score available and 10 is an average score. Todd scored 19 on three subtests and 18 on another subtest. Greg scored 7 and Todd

TABLE 1
WISC-III Index Scores

	Index Scores			
	Greg		Todd	
Verbal Comprehension	140	99.6%	146	99.9%
Perceptual Organization	114	82%	105	63%
Processing Speed	72	3%	99	47%
Freedom From Distractibility	129	97%	134	99%

scored 5 on the Picture Arrangement Subtest, both exceptionally low. This subtest measures students' abilities to recognize the sequence of actions and events in a story. It indicates potential problems with sequencing, inability to plan logically, perceptional organization, and attention to detail. On the Coding Subtest Greg scored 5 and Todd scored 7. The Coding Subtest measures visual-motor dexterity and can indicate short-term memory and fine motor problems. Greg's score of 4 on the Symbol Search Subtest could indicate problems with short-term memory (Nicholson & Alcorn, 1994). These low scores are significant and negatively influenced both students' school achievement.

EXECUTIVE FUNCTIONING

The executive control center of the brain located in the frontal lobe controls planning, judgment, attention, working memory, impulse control, self-regulation, and self-evaluation (Webb et al., 2005). The development of executive functioning often lags behind intelligence in gifted and twice-exceptional students. Many twice-exceptional learners can conceptualize advanced ideas, but weaknesses in planning, prioritizing, attention, organizing, and self-regulation make it difficult for them to manage assignments. As a result, they frequently fail to turn in assignments on time and receive a lower grade even though they have mastered the course content. It is important that teachers understand that gifted students can have weaknesses in executive functioning, which make it difficult for them to plan, prioritize, and organize their projects and homework.

Executive functioning is involved in planning, organizing, and self-regulation. It plays an important role in metacognition, higher order thinking, and problem solving. Students who have weaknesses in executive functioning struggle with planning, prioritizing, or managing time. They are the students with cluttered notebooks, backpacks, desks, and lockers. Everyone knows these students have great ideas, but they just cannot complete assignments in a timely manner. Because these students do not know how to prioritize, they can lose track of time working on an assignment that is due in a month when they have assignments due the next day. Coordinating multiple tasks is hard for students with weaknesses in executive functioning, and working memory deficits can further complicate the situation. Weaknesses in self-monitoring or self-correcting and in reflective thinking make it hard for students to figure out what went wrong when they are unable to complete assignments by the due date.

Homework Problems

Todd could conceptualize advanced ideas, but weaknesses in planning, prioritizing, attention, organizing, and self-regulation made it difficult for him to manage assignments. He could demonstrate mastery of the course content, but incomplete assignments lowered his grades. Teachers thought he was not acting responsibly and pressured him to become a more responsible student. He hated doing the drill and practice assignments on concepts he had mastered. Todd complained that his teachers were only concerned that he complete assignments on time. According to Todd's mother, the "teacher's insistence, 'You need to do these 90 problems; they need to all be legible and turned in every day' brought out his defiance—'Make me!'—and believe me you won't." He assumed the attitude, "It is OK, you can be as mean to me all you want, and do whatever you want, but you can't make me do it."

Todd was failing fifth grade, but he was getting A's in the college-level courses he was taking at the local community college. His mom said, "He did well in college courses because you get a syllabus with the assignments, and there are not as many of them. It is generally not lots of little minutia and daily work." The student's grade on the midterm and a final determined his grade, a benefit for Todd, as his mother noted:

> That plays to his strength. The minutia destroys him. When the minutia
> has become so important, that it is, say, three quarters of the grade, then
> it is devastating. However, when he was in a setting where the minutia
> didn't exist, he did well.

Todd worked to improve his skills when teachers respected his unique characteristics, provided challenging learning opportunities, focused on his strengths, and encouraged him to develop the skills he needed to be successful with positive reinforcement.

Todd's defiant attitude toward homework was not an isolated instance and highlights important issues. First, many gifted learners are not challenged in school and they rebel when forced to complete drill and practice assignments over material they have already mastered. The purpose of assignments are to provide practice so students will learn the content. If the students have mastered the content, they do not need to practice those skills. Second, assignments for gifted students must challenge them to develop critical/creative thinking and problem-solving skills. Gifted students need to study a topic in greater depth and complexity. Assignments should provide opportunities for them to apply what have learned in novel, relevant ways. Finally, these assignments motivate gifted students and require them to develop executive functioning and management skills. Be sure to teach time management and organizational skills. Provide scaffolding in the form of graphic organizers so they can monitor their progress and require students to reflect on how well they managed the assignment when the project is completed. Technology can reduce the impact of disabilities, allowing students to focus on the complex, creative, and analytical aspects of assignments. Twice-exceptional students need encouragement to use their advanced knowledge, abstract thinking, reasoning skills, and creativity in discussions, challenging projects, and real-world assignments (Baum et al., 2001).

Metacognitive Thinking

Cognition and metacognition are intertwined and closely dependent upon each other. Metacognitive thinking encompasses both the awareness of how students learn and how they manage the learning process. Learning metacognitive strategies will help students improve their executive functioning skills. As students become aware of how they learn, they begin to take conscious control of their learning. The metacognitive process includes awareness, planning, implementation, and reflection. It is important for students to learn how to set goals, plan effectively, implement their plan, monitor their progress in attaining the desired outcome, and reflect on the outcome. As students learn to examine the effectiveness of their planning, organization, and time management, they begin to see how they can change their approach in order to achieve their goals (Ridley, Schutz, Glanz, & Weinstein, 1992). The components of metacognitive thinking are summarized below:

The components of metacognitive thinking include the following:

- Awareness
  - What is the problem?
  - What is my goal?
  - What do I already know and what do I need to learn?
  - What are my available resources?

- Planning
  - What steps do I need to complete to achieve my goal?
  - What is the priority of each step? How long do I think each step will take to complete?
  - How can I develop a schedule to get each step completed?

- Implementation
  - Am I making adequate progress?
  - Will I be able to achieve my goal?
  - Do I need to make changes in order to successfully complete the project?

- Reflect
  - Did I achieve my goal?
  - Does the finished project represent quality work?
  - Was the project completed within the scheduled time?
  - What would I do differently next time?

Empower twice-exceptional learners by teaching them to use metacognitive strategies to manage their homework. When a metacognitive approach to instruction is used, students learn to take control of their own learning (Coleman, 2005). Teachers activate the students' prior knowledge to help them build conceptual frameworks for ideas and to assist students' in developing self-regulatory approaches to learning (Coleman, 2005), while at the same time providing explicit instruction relative to students' weaknesses (Barton & Starnes, 1989; Baum et al., 1989; Baum & Owen, 1988; Whitmore & Maker, 1985). Graphic organizers are visual devices that can guide students in developing metacognitive thinking. The graphic organizers included in the next section may be helpful for students. Coach students in developing metacognitive skills, but do not require students to use specific organizers. Let them choose the tools that work best for them.

Metacognitive planning and organization. Using metacognitive strategies will help twice-exceptional learners to plan, organize, and manage their time more effectively so they become more productive. Kara began each day frantically trying to find her books and homework. Often she would leave home without breakfast or the books, supplies, or homework she needed for the day. Learning to spend time at the end of each day preparing for the next day made a big difference. She spent time organizing her backpack with all of the books, papers, and homework assignments needed. The backpack was placed beside the front door so she could grab it as she left in the morning. She kept track of how much time it took in the morning to get ready for school, and she reduced the time by deciding the night before what she would wear. Now she was able to arrive at school on time with what she needed.

The metacognitive strategies listed below can improve students' planning and organizational skills. I've written them so that you can give these suggestions directly to students.

Tasks To-Do Today Date:_____	Prioritize	Completed

Figure 13. Sample to-do list organizer.

1. During the day, keep a to-do list of things you need to accomplish. Use the list in Figure 13 or make a to-do list on your computer, iPod, or other device.
2. Use the assignment organizer in Figure 14 or a paper or computerized calendar to:
    a. organize your assignments according to due dates, and
    b. plan what needs to be accomplished each day to complete the assignment by the due date.
3. The Long-Term Assignment Organizer in Figure 15 is helpful in planning long-term assignments.
4. Effective time management is critical to successful completion of homework.
    a. Record how you spend your time using Figure 16.
    b. Reflect on how you spent your time.
    c. Determine where you need to increase or decrease time.
    d. Continue until you have an appropriate schedule. Be sure to designated time for homework, school activities, and fun activities with family and friends.
5. Managing study time:
    a. Review your to-do list.
    b. Prioritize the list in order of importance.

    c. Estimate how long it will take to complete each task.

    d. Time yourself to determine the actual time it took to complete the task.

    e. Compare the estimated time with actual time.

    f. Check off each task as it is completed and celebrate.

    g. Take time to reflect on homework to determine how the process can be improved.

6. Homework folder:

    a. Keep homework in a separate folder.

    b. Place new assignments on the left side and completed assignments on the right side.

    c. Arrange completed assignments in the order of your classes.

    d. Take the folder out and place it on your desk at the beginning of the class.

    e. Before you leave class, check to make sure you handed in the assignment, add the new assignment, and put the folder in your backpack or bag.

    f. Before leaving school at the end of the day, check again to make sure you turned in every assignment.

7. In the evening before going to bed:

    a. Organize your backpack or school bag and place it in a prominent place so you can easily grab it as you leave in the morning.

    b. Decide what you are going to wear and place it on a chair in your room.

Reflect on the day considering what went right, what went wrong, and what changes you will make tomorrow.

Long-Term Assignment Organizer. The organizer in Figure 15 will assist students in developing organizational, time management, and metacognitive skills. Use the organizer to guide whole-class or small-group discussions of how to organize a long-term assignment. With this knowledge, students are able to organize their own projects and develop self-regulation skills. The organizer requires students to:

1. List the steps needed to complete the assignment.
2. Estimate how long they think each step will take.
3. Assign a completion date for each step. Consider how long each step takes and work backward from the due date to determine when each step must be completed so the project is finished on time.
4. Keep track of the actual time it takes to complete each step.
5. Compare estimated time to actual time: Did they do a good job of estimating how long the assignment would take?
6. Reflect: Did they finish the assignment on time? What problems did they experience? What steps were they able to accomplish without problems? Next time what would they do differently?

Assignment Organizer for Monday _____ to Friday _____ Name_____		Due Date	Prioritize	Estimate how long it will take.	How long did it take to complete?
Monday					
Tuesday					
Wednesday					
Thursday					
Friday					

Figure 14. Assignment organizer.

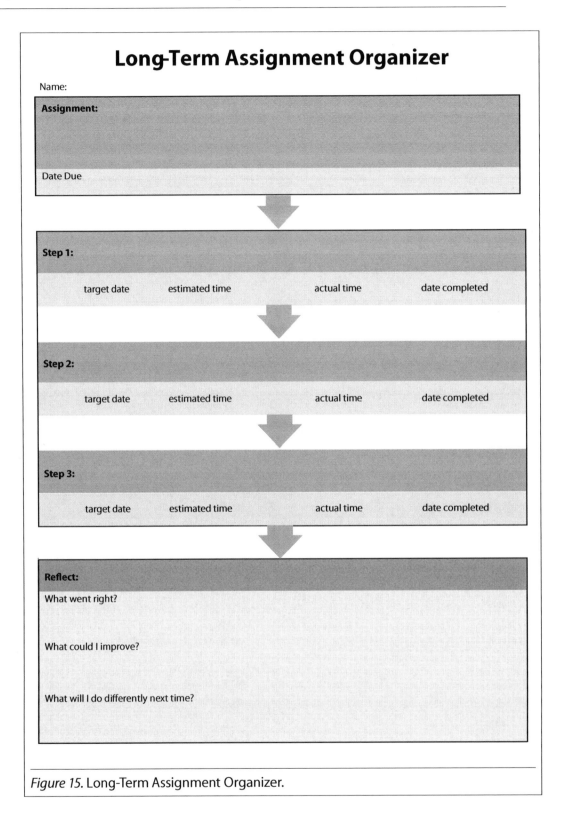

Figure 15. Long-Term Assignment Organizer.

Time Management

Time	Task	(I)ncrease or (D)ecrease time by ___ minutes	Proposed Schedule
5–6 a.m.			
6–7 a.m.			
7–8 a.m.			
8–9 a.m.			
9–10 a.m.			
10–11 a.m.			
11 a.m.–12 p.m.			
12–1 p.m.			
1–2 p.m.			
2–3 p.m.			
3–4 p.m.			
4–5 p.m.			
5–6 p.m.			
6–7 p.m.			
7–8 p.m.			
8–9 p.m.			
9–10 p.m.			
10–11 p.m.			
11 p.m.–12 a.m.			

Figure 16. Time Management Chart.

Executive functioning strategies. These strategies will help students to learn how to prioritize and organize their homework assignments:

- Teach students how to use a to-do list, prioritize assignments, predict how long it will take to complete the assignment, and compare the predicted to actual time.
- Encourage them to use a two-sided folder for homework. Students should place homework they need to do in the left side of the folder and completed assignments that need to be turned in each day on the right side.
- Post assignments online so students and parents can access it at home. Provide an assignment drop box for students to submit assignments on the class web page or allow them to e-mail the assignment to the teacher.
- Use the Long-Term Assignment Organizer in Figure 15 to teach students how to break down long-term assignments into short segments of work, estimate the time it will take to complete each step, and set a target date for completion of each step.

ATTENTION

Students' abilities to maintain attention clearly influences their learning and information processing. Students with attention problems are inattentive and easily distracted by sounds or movement. They have difficulty staying on task and can behave impulsively. It is hard for them to focus and sustain attention. Gifted children have characteristics similar to children with Attention Deficit/ Hyperactivity Disorder (ADHD), and they can be incorrectly diagnosed with attention problems when they are not attentive (Hartnett, Nelson, & Rinn, 2004). "Inattention in the classroom may also occur when children with high intelligence are placed in academically understimulating environments" (American Psychiatric Association [APA], 2000, p. 91). ADHD is characterized by the core symptoms of inattention, impulsivity, and hyperactivity.

Inattention

The inability to stay focused and attend to mundane tasks is characteristic of inattention. Irrelevant sounds (the aquarium pump) or sights (flickering florescent light) may easily distract students. These students have a difficult time with selective attention, which is their capacity to focus awareness on a selected stimuli such as classroom instruction. The more proficient a student is at screening out unimportant sounds and sights, the easier it is for him to focus his attention on the important tasks. Gifted children in heterogeneously grouped classrooms can spend more than half of their time waiting for others to catch up (Gallagher & Harradine, 1997). For example, Greg complained about having to spend so much time in school hearing about things he already knew. As a result, he became inattentive and tuned out during classroom instruction. He missed important information he needed to know because he was not paying attention. Students with attention problems can have a difficult time organizing and completing tasks. It is hard for them to determine what is relevant and what is not. They live life in a disorganized way and are described as forgetful or spacey when they lack time management and organizational skills.

Hyperactivity and Impulsivity

Many gifted students are reported to have high levels of energy, and they seem to be in constant motion. Even as infants they require less sleep and this trend continues throughout their life, with some only needing 4 or 5 hours of sleep each night (Webb, Meckstroth, & Tolan, 1982). A precocious verbally gifted child can be very intense and demonstrate some of the same behaviors as hyperactivity. Students with hyperactivity have a difficult time keeping their bodies still; they squirm, fidget, and move excessively. They interrupt others, talk excessively, and monopolize the conversation. This trait also is common in verbally gifted children. Hyperactive children have a difficult time regulating their activity level, which can lead to problems in the school environment. It is extremely difficult for them to contain their excessively high levels of activity and sit quietly in their chair to listen to instructions or complete assignments. Impulsive children act or speak out without considering the consequences. They forget to raise their hand and simply blurt out the answer. Waiting for their turn can be extremely difficult for these gifted children.

Diagnosing ADHD

The Conners' Parent and Teacher Rating Scales–Revised (Conners, 1997) is frequently used to diagnose ADHD. Psychologists and psychiatrists also use the APA's (2000) *Diagnostic and Statistical Manual of Mental Disorders, Fourth Edition, Text Revision* (DSM-IV-TR) to help diagnose ADHD (see Figure 17). Both require a teacher and/or parents to rate the child's behavior. However, parents and teachers should *not* try to diagnose a child on their own, but should seek professional help from a school psychologist or trained private psychiatrist.

Differentiating Between Gifted Behavior and Attention Problems

Differentiating between gifted behaviors and ADHD continues to be difficult. Unfortunately, many gifted children are misdiagnosed (Baum, Olenchak, & Owen, 1998). Scientists are using functional neuroimaging techniques to study

A. Either (1) or (2):

1.   six (or more) of the following symptoms of **inattention** have persisted for at least 6 months to a degree that is maladaptive and inconsistent with developmental level:

Inattention
  a.   often fails to give close attention to details or makes careless mistakes in schoolwork, work, or other activities
  b.   often has difficulty sustaining attention in tasks or play activities
  c.   often does not seem to listen when spoken to directly
  d.   often does not follow through on instructions and fails to finish schoolwork, chores, or duties in the workplace (not due to oppositional behavior or failure to understand instructions
  e.   often has difficulty organizing tasks and activities
  f.   often avoids, dislikes, or is reluctant to engage in tasks that require sustained mental effort (such as schoolwork or homework)
  g.   often loses things necessary for tasks or activities (e.g., toys, school assignments, pencils, books, or tools)
  h.   is often easily distracted by extraneous stimuli
  i.   is often forgetful in daily activities

2.   six (or more) of the following symptoms of **hyperactivity-impulsivity** have persisted for at least 6 months to a degree that is maladaptive and inconsistent with developmental level:

Hyperactivity
  a.   often fidgets with hands or feet or squirms in seat
  b.   often leaves seat in classroom or in other situations in which remaining seated is expected
  c.   often runs about or climbs excessively in situations in which it is inappropriate (in adolescents or adults, may be limited to subjective feelings of restlessness
  d.   often has difficulty playing or engaging in leisure activities quietly
  e.   is often "on the go" or often acts as if "driven by a motor"
  f.   often talks excessively

Impulsivity
  g.   often blurts out answers before questions have been completed
  h.   often has difficulty awaiting turn
  i.   often interrupts or intrudes on others (e.g., butts into conversations or games)

Figure 17. Diagnostic criteria for ADHD (APA, 2000, p. 92).

areas of the brain associated with attention. However, functional imaging is not accepted in the diagnosis of ADHD at this time, but may in time advance to a point where it can be clinically useful (Bush, 2008). Those wanting to differentiate between ADHD and gifted behaviors should examine the context of the behavior and attention problems in relation to these environmental factors: (a) children in new situations may not demonstrate ADHD behaviors until the novelty wears off; (b) children with ADHD need limits, structure, and routine, and gifted children will resist structure unless the situation is stimulating; (c) if interrupted, children with ADHD will have a difficult time refocusing, whereas gifted children will return with little prompting; and (d) at home, gifted children will focus on tasks of interest for long periods of time (Webb et al., 2005).

Strategies for Students With ADHD

- Provide a predictable routine and clear structure for students. Post the class schedule so students can refer to it when necessary. Let students know ahead of time when you are going to change the schedule.

- Alert students when a transition time is approaching. Doing a countdown or dimming the lights is an effective way to inform students a transition is approaching.

- Include students in developing classroom rules; post the rules in clear view. Provide preferential seating close to the teacher and away from distractions.

- Plan 20-minute instructional segments and include different kinds of activities. The schedule should incorporate movement, frequent breaks, and physical activities to reduce mental fatigue. Vary the pace of instruction throughout the day.

- Chunk new learning into manageable subtasks and relate it to previously learned information. Utilize graphic organizers, cue-sheets, flowcharts, or webs to help students make connections.

- List on the board the materials students will need for instruction so the students have time to find what they need.

- Begin the lesson by talking about learning and behavior expectations. Talk about what the students will learn and if it will be a group activity where they can talk quietly or individual work.

- Recognize when students are losing focus and cue them by touching their shoulders or placing a sticky note on their desks to remind them to focus. Squeezing a soft ball will help students to stay focused.

- Coach students in the use of metacognitive and self-regulation strategies to monitor their attention like: (a) lean the upper body forward toward the speaker while listening, (b) watch as well as listen by keeping your eyes on the speaker, and (c) when you notice your mind is wondering, refocus your attention.

- At the end of the lesson briefly summarize the important points. Provide both verbal and written instructions for assignments. Having assignments available on the web and a drop box for students to turn them into is helpful.

PROCESSING SPEED

Processing speed is an innate component of individual differences and is reflective of how fast information is processed in the brain. Many twice-exceptional learners experience problems with processing speed. It simply takes them longer to do things. They are moving in slow motion while others are functioning at full speed. These students can talk at a slower speed and sometimes pause to find the right words. Their writing, reading, and thinking speed is slower. More think time is needed before these students can respond to questions, but their slower processing speed does not affect the quality of their answers. Students with slow processing speed need more time to perform perceptual or cognitive tasks like understanding spoken directions, responding to questions, completing homework assignments, and so on. It is not a matter of intelligence, but a processing problem related to deficits in either auditory or visual processing. Students with slower processing speed just think and work at a slower pace. As a result, they can easily become overwhelmed with the amount of homework. These students perform poorly when trying to cope with implied or expressed time pressures.

Samantha felt overwhelmed and frustrated by middle school. She spent hours working on her homework assignments, but just could not seem to get everything done. Extended time for assignments did not work for her because it just meant she was accumulating more and more assignments that were past due. She became very emotional as her grades began to decline. The Wechsler Intelligence Scale for Children revealed Samantha's verbal comprehension was in the 98th percentile but her processing speed was at the 27th percentile. On the Woodcock-Johnson Test of Achievement, her fluency scores in reading, writing, and math were 50 percentile points below passage comprehension, writing sample, and calculations. With the implementation of strategies for slow processing speed, her grades improved along with her disposition.

Strategies for Students With Slow Processing Speed

- Students with slow processing speed need extra time to do everything but giving them extra time can create problems. A preferred approach would be to use the Most Difficult First strategy. This strategy allows students to complete a few of the most difficult problems first. If the students demonstrate mastery, they do not need further practice and do not need to complete the rest of the assignment.

- Assess students to find out what they already know before beginning instruction and compact the curriculum so students can skip the parts of the curriculum they know and instead study a topic of interest in greater detail or progress through the remaining curriculum at their own rate.

- Having an Individualized Education Program (IEP) with an accommodation for extra time is important for students planning to take the ACT or SAT for college admission, so they can qualify for extended time on these tests.

- Mastering computer keyboarding, word processing, and using spell/grammar checkers is helpful for students who lack writing fluency and/or cannot remember spelling and grammar rules.

- Implement interventions designed to increase reading, writing, and math fluency. Allow students to monitor their own progress by charting their growth in fluency. Computer fluency programs will be successful with most twice-exceptional learners. Utilize a reward system where students earn points for increases in fluency that they can use to purchase time to do an activity of their choice.

SENSORY INTEGRATION

Sensory integration is the neurological process by which the brain organizes and interprets sensory information. The brain receives and processes information from the five sensory systems (sight, sound, smell, taste, and touch) to develop an understanding of the environment (Ayres, 1972). It develops naturally in most children through sensory experiences as they interact with the environment and learn to adapt to incoming sensations. However, for some children sensory integration does not develop as efficiently as it should. When sensory integration dysfunction occurs, the brain is not able to process sensory information proficiently. A noisy environment, moderate visual stimulus, or strong tastes and smells can easily overwhelm children with sensory integration dysfunction. Even though they have perfect vision, some children may constantly bump into things because they are unaware of where their body is in relationship to space. They may experience problems when using scissors and may have a difficult time keeping inside the lines when coloring. Problems with muscle tone, coordination, and motor planning can lead to poor athletic ability (Kranowitz, 1998).

Some children are hyposensitive while others are hypersensitive. Hyposensitive children are constantly crashing into things because they seek extra stimulation. Hypersensitive children are supersensitive to touch, and they avoid being touched or touching anything. These students often complain about tags in clothing, seams in socks, or the texture of the material. The following are some characteristics of hypersensitivity and hyposenstivity:

- Hypersensitivity (Defensiveness)
  - Did not like to be held or cuddled as an infant and may arch back and pull away.
  - Can become fearful, anxious, or aggressive with light or unexpected touch.
  - Refuses to wear clothing with course texture and bothered by rough bed sheets.
  - Dislikes getting hands dirty or taking part in messy play with sand, mud, glue, or playdough.

- Can be a picky eater, avoiding certain tastes, textures, or temperatures of food.
- Hates to have face washed, hair brushed, or teeth brushed.
- May refuse to walk barefoot or may walk on toes.

- Hyposensitivity (Underresponsive)
  - Need to touch everything and enjoys messy play.
  - Repeatedly touches surfaces or objects that are soothing.
  - Not aware of being touched or bumped unless it is done with extreme force.
  - May be self-abusive such as biting, pinching, or banging head.
  - Frequently hurts other children when playing
  - Craves excessively spicy, sweet, sour, or salty food.

When their senses are overloaded, children with sensory integration dysfunction often experience a meltdown or tantrum. Understanding and managing these emotional outbursts can be difficult. Dysfunction in sensory integration makes it difficult for the child to modulate, discriminate, and coordinate sensations and movement. Children experiencing sensory integration problems have oversensitivity or underreactivity to touch, movement, sight, or sound. Their activity level can be unusually high or unusually low. They can appear clumsy, careless, and impulsive. It is difficult for them to make transitions and they are not able to unwind or calm themselves. Two systems play a role in sensory integration and motor planning—vestibular and proprioceptive.

Vestibular System

The vestibular system tells us where our body is in relation to space. It monitors our movement and sense of balance that is processed in the inner ear (DiMatties & Sammons, 2003). Problems in the vestibular system can lead to seeking or avoiding movement. Seeking movements include running, crashing, and twirling. Avoidance is seen in children who are afraid of falling so they avoid climbing, swinging, or riding a bike. You might see the following behaviors in relation to students who seek or avoid sensations:

- Sensory Seeking Behaviors
  - Stomps feet when walking
  - Seeks jumping, bumping, and crashing activities
  - Loves "roughhousing," tackling, and wrestling games
  - Frequently hits, bumps, or pushes other children
  - Chews on objects like pencils, pens, straws, etc.

- Sensory Avoiding Behaviors
  - Dislikes playing on swings, ladders, slides, or merry-go-rounds

- Moves slowly and cautiously and avoids taking risks
- Afraid of heights and prefers to keep feet on the ground
- Dislikes going up or down stairs and walking on uneven surfaces
- May appear clumsy and loses balance easily

Proprioception System

The proprioception system senses where the body parts are and provides information on what they are doing (DiMatties & Sammons, 2003). Tactile-proprioceptive perception refers to sensation of touch and body position. It plays a role in holding a pencil for writing. Vestibular-proprioceptive perception informs the brain on the body's position when moving. Knowing where the body is in relationship to the environment is necessary for activities like catching and throwing a ball. Proprioceptive activities for students who need and crave them include heavy work activities to help the body process movement and touch. These activities increase attention, arousal level, body awareness, and muscle tone, and decrease defensiveness.

Sensory Diet

The goal of sensory integration therapy is to provide a sensory diet where students experience a variety of tactile, vestibular, and proprioceptive input in a way that provides just the right challenge to promote increasingly more complex adaptive responses to environmental challenges. Therapy varies based on the students' needs. Occupational therapists create a "menu" of activities for children with sensory integration dysfunction and supervise the implementation of the plan. The following lists provide examples of some of the activities that may be used in sensory integration therapy.

Proprioception activities to develop body awareness include:

- heavy work activities such as carrying a heavy object or a backpack with books;
- pushing or pulling activities like pushing a shopping cart, pulling a wagon, mopping the floor, vacuuming, shoveling snow, or raking leaves;
- sandwich or squishing activities that provide firm overall pressure such as wrapping in a blanket, squashing between pillows, or giving a firm hug;
- squeezing or pinching an object like a soft ball or stress ball; and
- wearing weighted objects such as wrist or ankle weights, weighted vests, lap pads, or weighted blankets.

Vestibular activities to improve movement and balance include:

- rocking in a rocking chair;
- swinging on a swing;

- running, jumping, or skipping;
- spinning, rolling somersaults, cartwheels, and dancing;
- playing on seesaws and teeter totters; and
- bouncing on a therapy ball.

Tactile activities to aid in processing touch sensation include:
- playing with playdough, shaving cream, fingerpaint, stickers, rubber toys, water, rice, beans, and sand;
- painting or drawing using an easel;
- washing windows and wiping down a shower or tub; and
- using clothespins, spray bottles, scissors, rolling pin, and paper punches.

Auditory activities to enhance auditory processing include:
- playing rhythm on a drum, tambourine, or musical instruments;
- listening to music and games where students guess the sound;
- playing computer games with sounds; and
- clapping in unison, rhymes, repeating phrases, and saying tongue twisters.

Visual activities to enhance visual processing include:
- stringing beads,
- matching cards or matching words to pictures, and
- picture games and "I spy" books or game.

The following story will help you to understand what is it like to be a child with sensory integration problems.

Michael is a third grade student who is waiting for the school bus. He is challenged by sensory experiences during everyday activities that most of us don't even think about. While he's still reeling from the battle with mom over brushing his teeth (that peppermint toothpaste tastes like fire in his mouth) the school bus pulls up. Michael runs past the bus monitor's haze of perfume and sits at the back of the bus. In his heightened state, he becomes even more aware of his new school shirt with its stiff label and that awful feeling like a wire brush being poked into the back of his neck. The sensory experiences of the movement of the bus, the sound of his excited classmates laughing and yelling above the roar of the bus engine all contribute to his increased agitation. By the time Michael arrives at school he is wound up and ready to unravel. There is no time to wait for the bus monitor's direction . . . getting off the bus quickly becomes a matter of survival and he resorts to pushing, shoving and finally kicking his way out. Unfortunately, there is a price to pay for this seemingly outward aggression . . . he can expect another trip to the principal's office. (DiMatties & Sammons, 2003, p. 1).

Strategies for Students With Sensory Integration Issues

- In the early elementary grades, provide opportunities for students to experience a varied sensory diet.

- Watch for students who demonstrate sensory seeking or avoidance behaviors and those who may be hypersensitive or hyposensitive. Ask an occupational therapist to screen those students for sensory integration dysfunction.

- Have a quiet place or tent in the classroom where students can go if they begin to feel overwhelmed and need some quiet time. Pillows, beanbags, and sleeping bags have a calming effect.

- Take a 5–10-minute quiet break, play soft music, and dim or turn off lights.

- Pushing activities, carrying a weighted item, and weighted blankets or lap pads are calming activities.

- Students who are hypersensitive to touch should be the last in line.

- Squeezing a soft ball or rubbing a smooth stone can be calming and help students focus on classroom instruction.

- Slowing down your speech and using a soft voice is calming. A louder voice and quickened pace in your speech is alerting.

- Decrease distractions by removing visual clutter or distracting noises for students who are hypersensitive to sound and visual stimuli.

- Prearrange an activity that can be quickly implemented if a student becomes overstimulated. The activity could be carrying, pushing, or pulling a heavy box from one location to another or taking a sack full of books to the library.

SUMMARY

Cognitive disabilities diminish the brain's ability to process information. These hidden disabilities can cause children to struggle when learning to read, write, and memorize math facts, and they limit their ability to sustain attention or remember verbal instructions. Auditory processing deficits can cause difficulty in decoding words, spelling, and sentence structure. These learners have a hard time following oral direction and learning from lectures. Visual processing problems can affect reading comprehension and students' ability to copy information from the board. Deficits in visual motor coordination and sequential processing can cause problems with handwriting. A sequential processing weakness influences reading speed and fluency along with the ability to sound out words or remember formulas and steps. Executive functioning affects the learner's ability to plan, organize, and prioritize. Learners with difficulties in this area struggle to coordinate multiple tasks simultaneously. Slower processing speed results in problems with short- and long-term memory retrieval when time pressures are in place. Students' hyper- or hyposensitivity to their environments may affect their ability to learn and behave.

Chapter 6

ENCOURAGING ACADEMIC ACHIEVEMENT

Hidden disabilities can cause gifted children to struggle when learning to read, write, or memorize math facts and can limit their ability to sustain attention or remember verbal instructions. It was not until the 1970s that researchers and educators began to discuss the potential of gifted students having disabilities. Maker (1977) hypothesized that the incidence of giftedness should occur at the same rate in the population of students with disabilities as it did in the population of students without disabilities, estimating that 3% of students with disabilities were also gifted. Today there are still some educators who believe gifted students cannot have disabilities. However, learning disorders can occur in almost any area of brain functioning (Webb et al., 2005). Disabilities in gifted students are frequently overlooked and optimum times for intervention are missed. Early identification of learning deficits and specific interventions are needed for these students to overcome their deficits. However, focusing on their deficits can lead to underachievement, so it is imperative that interventions are planned to provide challenging learning opportunities related to students' areas of strength while providing explicit instruction and support in their areas of weakness. This chapter will discuss underachievement and provide strategies to promote academic achievement. It will include strength-based interventions for reading, writing, and math along with explicit interventions for dyslexia, dysgraphia, and dyscalculia.

Underachievement

Hidden disabilities and inappropriate educational conditions contribute to the underachievement of twice-exceptional learners (Reis & McCoach, 2002). Underachievement in gifted students is considered by some to be an oxymoron. Many believe that gifted students are supposed to be the students who achieve in school. However, as many as 50% of gifted students do not perform up to their potential (Hoffman, Wasson, & Christianson, 1985). There are multiple definitions of underachievement cited in the research on gifted students. In most instances the definition describes a discrepancy between potential and actual achievement. Twice-exceptional learners can be more prone to underachievement because of their asynchronous development and inconsistent academic performance. These students often are out of sync with the school curriculum and are likely to be perceived as underachievers by teachers who do not understand how hidden disabilities can prevent gifted students from achieving. They often are seen as gifted students who have outstanding potential, but are lazy and choose not to work up to their potential. However, twice-exceptional learners have exceptional potential for contributions to society that will be lost if steps are not taken to prevent and reverse underachievement.

Underachievement can begin for twice-exceptional learners when the curriculum is not sufficiently challenging. Twice-exceptional learners need challenging learning opportunities just like other gifted students. When the curriculum is not challenging, they can lose their motivation and disengage from school. A study by the United States Department of Education, *National Excellence: A Case for Developing America's Talent* (1993), reported that many gifted and talented elementary students had mastered 35%–50% of the curriculum before the school year began. Gifted students can coast through the beginning years of school. In the process, they may learn to expect good grades with little effort.

Underachievement can result when teachers try to fix twice-exceptional learners and the focus of interventions becomes remediation (Reis & McCoach, 2002). Unfortunately some teachers will focus on their students' weaknesses and pay little attention to their strengths. When teachers focus on fixing twice-exceptional students, the results can be defiant behavior, depression, loss of motivation, underachievement, and lowered self-esteem. Research has shown that it is not good practice to focus on weaknesses because it results in poor self-esteem, lack of motivation, depression, and stress (Baum, 1984b; Whitmore & Maker, 1985).

In my observations, when teachers focused on the twice-exceptional students' weaknesses and ignored their strengths, it had a negative influence on their achievement, as Todd shared:

> I think the fact that I was ADHD and disorganized and things like that were really played up and made to be a huge deal as opposed to what I could do well. I think it [what he did well] was basically ignored a lot of the time.

He further commented:

> In fifth grade both of my teachers were just really into making you feel bad. You felt really bad every time you left the class. That was the problem I had with it. You had no desire to go home and learn because you felt anything you couldn't do was just highlighted and made really obvious. In my case, I had trouble with organization so it was made very obvious that I was having trouble. I had a friend who had trouble with reading and they would make a really big deal about that. So anything that was negative about what was happening was hammered home. That is what was left in your mind.

I asked him if this focus on his weaknesses influenced his motivation and he replied, "Definitely, I didn't have any interest in going home and doing homework. Tomorrow is not going to be any better if I do or I don't, so why bother?"

Teachers can provide the encouragement twice-exceptional learners need to learn to persist through their struggles. Greg and Todd achieved when teachers emphasized developing their strengths while at the same time providing explicit instruction relative to their weaknesses (Barton & Starnes, 1989; Baum et al., 1998; Baum & Owen, 1988; Whitmore & Maker, 1985). When gifted students are not challenged, they do not develop the discipline needed to be successful in a competitive world. In their minds, success is linked to intelligence, not to effort. At some point during their education they will encounter a course that will require them to invest effort in order to be successful. Will these gifted learners be able to handle the increasing demands to achieve success? Or, will they continue to underachieve and expect to get good grades? What will happen when they are not able to meet their own expectations and the expectations of others? According to Greg,

> I know that it is within my ability to just read the notes for an hour before the test and get an A on it. So, I don't do anything else. I know to

be successful at something you have to devote yourself to developing the skills you need. I never learned the discipline to put the right effort in.

Underachievement also can occur when assignments do not match the learning style of students. The twice-exceptional learner often understands the concepts but simply cannot manage large amounts of homework. Deficits in executive functioning skills decrease their ability to plan, prioritize, and manage assignments. Increases in the required homework as they progress into higher grades can cause some twice-exceptional learners to underachieve. Like most gifted students, they do not need drill and practice assignments in order to master a concept. They need assignments that match their learning style and allow them to apply what they have learned in creative, relevant ways. They crave opportunities to apply the knowledge they have learned as professionals would.

Twice-exceptional learners are motivated learners when allowed to generate unique ideas, produce creative solutions, and solve novel problems autonomously (Beckley, 1998; Whitmore & Maker, 1985). They needed opportunities to use their advanced knowledge, abstract thinking, reasoning skills, and creativity in discussions, challenging projects, and real-world assignments (Baum et al., 2001). For example, Todd became a defiant underachiever when teachers were rigid and required him to do things their way. However, he later eagerly completed a comparison study of Civil War battles that allowed him the freedom to study a topic of interest in greater depth when he was given the choice of this assignment over the class assignment to complete a report on an animal.

Underachievement is a learned behavior that can have devastating consequences. Unfortunately, many high school underachievers continue the pattern of underachievement after graduation. There is no research on dropout rates for twice-exceptional learners. However, it is well documented that twice-exceptional students are at risk in an education system that does not understand their inconsistent academic performance. Some drop out of high school and other choose not to further their education because the K–12 experience was so frustrating. As a result, they will never be able to develop their potential. Consider the fact that many of these students have incredible strengths, higher level thinking skills, and the creative ability needed to solve the world's most difficult problems, and the need to serve twice-exceptional students appropriately becomes even greater.

Promoting Academic Success

Gifted students need to be able to share their wealth of knowledge, inclination for advanced-level content, outstanding analytical ability (Barton & Starnes, 1989; Silverman, 1989; Whitmore & Maker, 1985), and complex problem-solving skills (Reis & Neu, 1994; Silverman, 1989; Whitmore & Maker, 1985;

Yewchuck, 1986). For example, when educators emphasize mastering the skills of practicing scientists, twice-exceptional students excel (Baum et al., 2001). Using inquiry methods, primary sources, and technology are other sophisticated ways of enhancing student learning. Field trips, films, television documentaries, and computer software related to required curriculum can provide alternative ways of learning content. Technology can reduce the impact of disabilities, allowing students to focus on the complex, creative, and analytical aspects of assignments. Twice-exceptional students need opportunities to use their advanced knowledge, abstract thinking, reasoning skills, and creativity in discussions and challenging projects (Baum et al., 2001).

Teachers can improve outcomes for twice-exceptional learners when they focus on the development of their strengths. When their strengths have been acknowledged, twice-exceptional learners are more receptive to working to develop the skills they need to be successful in the classroom. Teachers should determine what skill deficits are negatively impacting academic performance and provide explicit instruction on those skills. Incorporate organizational and time management skills into the classroom, and assist students in learning how to organize their papers, desk, backpack, and locker. Teach students different strategies they can use to keep track of homework assignments and prioritize what needs to be done. Use technology to augment learning and to promote productivity. Teachers must coach students who struggle with organization through long-term projects. Allow students to use compensatory strategies to bypass their challenge area.

FLUENCY AND AUTOMATICITY

Students with dyslexia, dysgraphia, and dyscalculia lack fluency and automaticity in reading, writing, and math computations. Most students develop fluency and automaticity naturally as they learn to read, write, and solve mathematical problems. However, some twice-exceptional learners continue to struggle with fluency and automaticity. Difficulties with automatic word recognition significantly reduce readers' abilities to comprehend what they have read. Fluent readers do not have to focus attention on decoding words; instead they can focus on the meaning. The lack of automaticity in writing can greatly reduce the student's ability to put her thoughts on paper. Fluent writers do not have to focus on the formation of each letter. As the brain learns to automate activities, one is able to complete multiple tasks at the same time. As a student practices a process, she becomes more proficient, and less active attention is required. When the reading and writing process is automated, the student can then focus her attention on the content.

Authors:	Hans Christian Anderson, Lewis Carrol
Inventors:	Alexander Graham Bell, Thomas Edison
Entertainers:	Tom Cruise, Whoopi Goldberg, Henry Winkler, Orlando Bloom, John Lennon, Steven Spielberg
Entrepreneurs:	Steve Jobs, Henry Ford, Charles Schwab, Ted Turner, Walt Disney, Richard Branson
Politicians:	Nelson Rockefeller, Sir Winston Churchill, Thomas Jefferson, Woodrow Wilson
Athletes:	Muhammad Ali, Bruce Jenner, Nolan Ryan, Magic Johnson
Artists	Pablo Picasso, Leonardo da Vinci, Ansel Adams
Nobel Prize Winners:	Albert Einstein, Pierre Curie, Sir William Bragg, Sir Lawrence Bragg, Sir Joseph Thomson, Sir George Thomson

Figure 18. Famous people with dyslexia.

READING AND DYSLEXIA

Dyslexia is an inherited neurologically based disorder that interferes with acquisition and processing of language. Individuals with dyslexia can experience extreme difficulty learning to read, write, and spell, despite the fact they may be exceptionally gifted. The degree of severity varies with individuals. Many famous people were diagnosed with dyslexia, but overcame their disability to achieve in their chosen field. The fact that they learned the valuable lesson of persistence may account for their success in later live. A few famous people with dyslexia are listed in Figure 18.

Studying these persons' stories in more depth can influence twice-exceptional learners to pursue their goals. For example, the work of William and Lawrence Bragg on X-ray crystallography was fundamental to understanding the structure of the DNA molecule that carries all genetic information. Patience Thomas, Lawrence Bragg's daughter, studied five generations of their family. Twelve members of the family were mildly dyslexic and 11 were dyslexic. Members of this family were strong visual thinkers with strengths in art design, computer graphics, mathematics, mechanics, or engineering. Although they had trouble with reading, spelling, arithmetic, rote memorization, and foreign language, they still made a significant contribution to genetic research.

Research on Dyslexia

Developmental dyslexia is related to language development but there is no consensus on the specific nature or causal factors of dyslexia (Lyytinen et al., 2004).

The ability to learn to read depends on the acquisition of a variety of skills. Dyslexia is attributed to deficiencies in visual perception and visual memory, language and linguistic skills, phonological coding, and low-level auditory processing (Vellutino, Fletcher, Snowling, & Scanlon, 2004). Students with deficits in any of these areas find it difficult to learn how to decode words and read with fluency. Decoding skills require (a) the acquisition of the letter sounds, (b) the subsequent training of the connections to a point of automatic retrieval from memory, and (c) the acquisition of phonemic assembly skills (Lyytinen et al., 2004).

Children from families with a history of dyslexia have a higher incidence of dyslexia. A longitudinal research study found differences between at-risk infants with a family history of dyslexia and control infants as early as a few days old (Lyytinen et al., 2004). At-risk infants processed sounds in the right hemisphere while children in the control group processed the sounds in the left hemisphere. By age 6 months, the at-risk infants had problems discriminating between various speech sounds. They continued to process auditory information in the right hemisphere, which interfered with their language developments (Lyytinen et al., 2004). This finding was supported by magnetic source imaging that showed different brain activation maps for children at risk for dyslexia and in adults. The majority of children with serious reading problems show a distinct brain activation profile (Papanicolaou et al., 2003). This atypical response continued at 6 months of age, when the children had a difficult time discriminating between sounds. This created a cascading effect on more advanced levels of phonological processing (Lyytinen et al., 2004). Children who could not distinguish between differences in speech sounds had a difficult time with decoding, accurate fluent reading, and comprehension. When the left temporoparietal region is not engaged, the ability to acquire reading skills is severely compromised (Papanicolaou et al., 2003).

Phoneme manipulation was closely associated with letter identification, letter sound knowledge, speech perception, and vocabulary (Mann & Foy, 2003). Their findings suggest a complex pattern of relationships, and all of these skills are involved in development of speech skills and phonological awareness. The ability to repeat unfamiliar words can be a predictor of subsequent dyslexia (Stein et al, 2004). Both auditory and visual processing along with timing and speed of processing were shown in studies to influence children's ability to learn to read. Phonological processing ability was linked to the child's verbal working memory performance (Kibby, Marks, Morgan, & Long, 2004). Problems with phonological awareness and verbal short-term memory are predictive of dyslexia and consistent with other studies (Stein et al., 2004).

The results of all studies support the need for early identification. Early interventions are critical for children at risk of dyslexia. The profiles of children with dyslexia may return to typical as a result of successful reading interventions (Papanicolaou et al., 2003). These studies indicate that it is possible to identify children who are at risk for dyslexia with relative accuracy at a very early age.

Parental reading problems are good indicators of children who will require preventative support (Lyytinen et al., 2004). Knowledge of letter sounds is predictive of phoneme manipulation (Mann & Foy, 2003). Rapid naming was found to be a significant predictor of reading problems at age 5. Helping the children acquire letter-sound associations, establish accurate phonemic perceptions, and automatize the retrieval and assembly of graphemes and phonemes may prevent the frustration and failure children with dyslexia experience during the first years of school (Lyytinen et al., 2004).

Monica was a high school sophomore taking Advanced Placement classes before her reading disability became an issue. Private testing revealed that she was only reading at a third-grade level. Amazingly, Monica had scored in the 86th percentile on the Iowa Tests of Basic Skills (ITBS) in reading when she was in ninth grade. I asked Monica how she was able to score so high on ITBS given her poor reading skills. She told me she would read the question first and the majority of the time was able to answer the question without reading the passage. If she did not know the answer, she scanned the text to find the correct answer. Monica was an excellent student who was able to disguise a reading disability and, as a result, optimum times for reading interventions were missed. Fortunately, systematic assessments of reading skills are making it more difficult for twice-exceptional students to hide their reading disabilities. It is less likely they will reach middle or high school before poor decoding and fluency makes it difficult for them to keep up with the volume of reading needed to be successful in school.

Learning to read can be a very frustrating experience for students with dyslexia, even though they may have exceptional verbal and communication skills. These twice-exceptional learners have low tolerance for frustration, dislike repetition and drill, and experience boredom with grade-level or below grade-level reading tasks (Hishinuma & Tadaki, 1996). They must have access to sophisticated materials and ideas as they work to improve deficit areas.

Strategies for Students With Dyslexia
- When children are struggling to learn to read, it becomes increasingly important for them to experience the excitement of the written words. They can develop this appreciation as they listen to a parent or teacher reading with expression, and in the process they learn skills that will help them to become better readers.
- Twice-exceptional learners need to understand that many famous people have dyslexia and have succeeded despite their struggles. See Figure 18 for a list to share with students.
- Even though twice-exceptional learners may struggle with learning to decode words, they need to be engaged in analyzing text using higher level thinking and complexity of thought.

- Provide alternate ways for students to access text material such as computers and text-to-speech software, books on tape, or choral reading.
- Engage twice-exceptional learners in high-level thinking, discussions of multiple perspectives, and exploring story elements. Literacy units developed by The College of William and Mary's Center for Gifted Education are recommended. For example, the center's *Jacob's Ladder* curriculum is effective at promoting high-level thinking, while its Navigator Units focus on story elements and help guide students in the exploration of plot, setting, theme, conflict, and climax (see http://www.cfge.wm.edu for more information).

Key elements of research-based reading interventions include improving classroom instruction and access to intensive explicit instruction. It is important to determine where the breakdown is occurring and provide instruction in that specific area. The intervention must match the student's level of reading development. Instruction should be explicit, systematic, and based on the needs of the learner. Students need direct explanations, teacher modeling, guided questioning, guided practice, and instruction linked to continuous assessment.

Phonological Awareness

Phonological awareness is the awareness of speech sounds that comprise the phonological structure of words. It is the ability to distinguish between the sounds of different syllables and phonemes. An important step in learning to read is recognizing that words are composed of phonemes (sounds) that can be segmented into syllables and manipulated to create new words.

Phonemic Awareness

Phonemic awareness is the ability to hear, identify, and manipulate phonemes, the smallest units of sound. Phonemic awareness instruction teaches students to manipulate phonemes and to blend or segment sounds in speech. Assessments used to determine phonemic awareness include the Test of Word Reading Efficiency (TOWRE) and the Dynamic Indicators of Basic Early Literary Success (DIBELS).

Strategies for Teaching Phonological and Phonemic Awareness
- Use multisensory engagement and model oral production of sounds and words (i.e., I do one, we do one, you do one). Teach students to hear each sound in words and to manipulate the sounds. Provide visual images of letters when teaching phoneme manipulation.

- The most effective phonemic awareness programs included "explicitly and systematically teaching children to manipulate phonemes with letters, focusing the instruction on one or two types of phoneme manipulations rather than multiple types, and teaching students in small groups" according to the National Institute of Child Health and Human Development (2000, p. 7).

Phonics

Early intervention with expert instruction is important for children with auditory processing problems who have trouble analyzing and synthesizing sounds. They cannot hear the differences in speech sounds or hear the words incorrectly. For example, instead of "spaghetti," they may hear "pisgetti." A reader with working memory problems may have trouble blending individual sounds into words or remembering the sounds of a word's first syllable.

Phonics instruction stresses the acquisition of letter-sound correspondences. This is the association of letters to corresponding sounds in language. It is an essential part of reading instruction to help "readers understand how letters are linked to sounds (phonemes) to form letter-sound correspondences and spelling patterns" according to the National Institute of Child Health and Human Development (2000, p. 8).

A meta-analysis by the National Institute of Child Health and Human Development (2000) found systematic phonics instruction produced significant benefits for K–6 students and students with reading disabilities. There were increases in students' abilities to read text orally and improvements in their capability to decode and spell words. Teachers should assess the needs of individual students and plan instruction to meet their individual needs. Teachers can assess the effectiveness of this phonics instruction using the DIBELS assessment or by keeping accurate, running records of cued and missed words.

Reading Fluency

Reading fluency is the ability to read quickly, accurately, and with expression. When reading is effortless and automatic with little conscious attention given to the mechanics of decoding, readers can focus their attention on understanding the text (Pikulski & Chard, 2005). Fluency is necessary for enjoyable reading and good comprehension. Reading at a slow, halting pace with frequent mistakes, poor phrasing, and inadequate intonation is characteristic of nonfluent reading. Early intervention is important in the areas of fluency and automaticity. Fluent readers enjoy reading and read more books. To be a fluent reader, the child must be able to recognize most of the words in a passage by sight.

Strategies for Reading Fluency Instruction

- Use a tracking device such as three fingers or a bookmark or slide a card over the text line-by-line from top to bottom.

- Have students read for one minute, count the number of words they read correctly, and record the score on a chart. If reading is slow and halting, complete a phonemic awareness assessment. Ask students to set a personal goal for the number of words they read in a minute. Continue the activity each day until the goal is met then celebrate the achievement of the student's goal.

- Focus on improving number of words read in specified time for each individual student.

- Read with students for 10–15 minutes per day. Read at a slightly faster pace than the students and encourage them to keep up.

- Select a passage of 50–100 words that is slightly above the student's independent reading level. Read for accuracy the first time and then repeat four times to develop fluency. Record speed and number of words pronounced incorrectly.

- Have a student read aloud and provide guidance as she reads. This Guided Oral Reading strategy has a significant, positive impact on word recognition, fluency, and comprehension across a range of grade levels.

Comprehension

Reading comprehension is an interaction between the reader and the text. Comprehension is fostered through thoughtful discussions of literature that require students to summarize, synthesize, analyze, and evaluate the ideas of the text. Gifted students with dyslexia should have an opportunity to participate in literature discussion groups with other gifted students. Record the text for these students or have them read at home with their parents prior to class discussion. Discussions with other gifted students will motivate students with reading difficulties to persist in overcoming their difficulties. If left in the lower reading group, gifted students will lose interest in reading.

Strategies for Teaching Reading Comprehension

- The College of William and Mary's Center for Gifted Education language arts curriculum (see the section on Strategies for Students With Dyslexia) and the Junior Great Books program both provide excellent opportunities for gifted learners to discuss literature while using their advanced thinking skills.

- Use high-interest reading material and teach comprehension strategies so students are able to monitor their understanding as they read.

- Encourage students to use sticky notes to write questions, note connections, or record relevant information as they read the text.
- Use color strips for categorizing information like philosophy statements and figures of speech.
- Provide graphic organizers such as story maps so students can visually record information as they read.
- Pose questions for students to answer as they read or ask students to generate questions as they read.
- Assignments should emphasize summarizing, organizing/categorizing, analyzing, synthesizing, and evaluating. Allow students who struggle with reading to use recorded versions of the book or text-to-speech software so they can participate in high-level discussions.

WRITING AND DYSGRAPHIA

Dysgraphia is a spectrum disorder describing major difficulties in mastering the sequence of movements necessary to write letters and numbers. Students with dysgraphia may also have problems with auditory and/or visual processing, fine motor coordination, executive functioning, kinesthetic monitoring system, working memory, procedural long-term memory, sequencing, and fluency. It can manifest as difficulties with spelling, poor handwriting, and trouble putting thoughts on paper. Students with dysgraphia experience difficulty mastering the sequence of movements necessary to write letters and numbers. Writing requires the coordination of the occipital, temporal, and frontal lobes of the brain; the motor and somatosensory cortex; and the cerebellum. Letter identification and visual processing occurs across the back of both hemispheres in the occipital lobe. The speech center, the Broca's area, is located in the temporal lobe. This lobe stores vocabulary, grammar, and syntax. Auditory and phonological processing occurs in the temporal lobe. The executive control center is located in the frontal lobe along with the working memory. It is responsible for planning, thinking, higher order thinking, and problem solving. The motor cortex coordinates the learning of motor skills. Touch signals from different parts of the body are processed in the somatosensory cortex. The cerebellum monitors timing of complex motor tasks and stores the memory of automatic movement. Mental rehearsal improves the sequence of movement, increases speed and accuracy, and reduces effort. Handwriting must become an automated process so students can focus their attention on the content, organization, grammar, and syntax of their work.

A marked discrepancy between the quality of ideas expressed in class discussions and what is produced on paper signal to teachers that something is impeding written expression. Writing is particularly difficult for some gifted students because it involves rapid, precise synchronization of multiple brain functions and thought processes. Students with graphomotor dysfunction have impaired coordination of the small muscles needed to form letters. There is a breakdown in the connection between the brain and the fingers, which makes writing slow and often illegible. Sometimes inadequate motor memory feedback causes students to have difficulty integrating motor output with memory input. They have difficulty with rapid, consistent recall of letter shapes, slowing the writing process. The pencil grip of students with graphomotor production deficits is unstable. Students may hold the pencil too close to the point, perpendicular to the page, and use extremely heavy pressure when writing. Students with motor feedback problems have difficulty tracking the exact location of the pencil point.

Occupational therapy is necessary for students who do not have the trunk, shoulder, arm, wrist, or finger control needed to write. Therapy sessions can provide the physical activity required to develop postural stability and upper body strength. Midline stability, dynamic forearm rotation, and wrist adjustment are important. The occupational therapist will combine activities to develop stable postural muscles and adequate trunk balance, including climbing structures, sandboxes, and tricycles. Activities to develop fine motor skills are comprised of wind-up toys, pop-beads, clothespins, tweezers, Tinkertoys, fingerpainting, and playing with clay or playdough.

Strategies for Improving Handwriting

- Help students to understand that writing is a complex process that takes practice. Explain how with practice the skill becomes automatic.
- When students write on a blackboard, the chalk in the fingertips provides feedback to the brain. Students must cross the midline as they write in large letters on the blackboard, which is helpful with midline stability and integration of the hemispheres of the brain.
- Practicing writing improves skills, so encourage students to write in a journal daily.
- Provide explicit instruction to improve handwriting and reward significant effort in writing. Have students practice writing letters and numbers in the air, on the board, in sand, in shaving cream, and on paper.
- Experiment with a variety of pencils and pens to find the one that works best. Practice using the normal tripod pencil grip and hold the pencil one half inch from the point. Use paper with raised lines to help the student stay on the line.
- Allow alternatives to written expression such as recording the assignment on a digital recorder or creating a PowerPoint presentation, poster, or other visual presentation of the information.

The writing process requires the simultaneous application of multiple memory functions. Twice-exceptional students have trouble coordinating the ideas that are flooding into their active memory with the handwriting process. Their handwriting cannot keep up with the ideas they are trying to express. Other students can have a difficult time organizing their thoughts. The resulting products often are sparse, primitive, and barely legible. It is easy to understand why a teacher would assume the student had invested little effort. The challenge for teachers is to support students in their efforts to develop the writing skills they need to be successful in school while not punishing them for not being able to put their thoughts on paper. Pair a creative student who has poor writing skills with a student who has good writing skills but may not have creative ideas. It is best if both students can contribute and benefit from the collaboration. Early introduction to the computer and word processing can help students compensate for lagging fine motor skills. Learning how to develop a PowerPoint presentation instead of writing a report is a good accommodation for twice-exceptional learners. With both tasks, students learn to organize their thoughts and express their ideas. Not only will the students learn compensatory skills but they also will develop lifelong skills.

Strategies for Overcoming Writing Difficulties

- Encourage the use of a computer and word processor to increase productivity. Grammar and spell checker is effective in eliminating grammar and spelling errors, allowing the student to focus on the content.

- Use voice recognition software like Dragon Naturally Speaking to convert spoken words into text on the computer. It works well for students who articulate their words carefully.

- Begin writing assignments with a creative activity such as drawing a cover page or creating a sequence of illustrations for the story.

- Brainstorm ideas and use graphic organizers like story maps (see Figure 19) or story webs (see Figure 20), so students can organize their thoughts before beginning the writing process.

MATH AND DYSCALCULIA

Dyscalculia is a learning disability where children have problems with mathematical computations. As preschoolers they may experience difficulties recognizing numbers and learning to count. They may struggle learning to tell time, handling money, and understanding word problems. Some students will have difficulties sequencing steps in the proper order while others will have problems remembering math facts. Gifted students with dyscalculia can have high verbal and creative abilities. Difficulty mastering math facts may result in students being excluded from higher mathematical problem-solving activities (Baum et al., 2001). However, gifted students have a low tolerance for rote-drill math tasks and often become

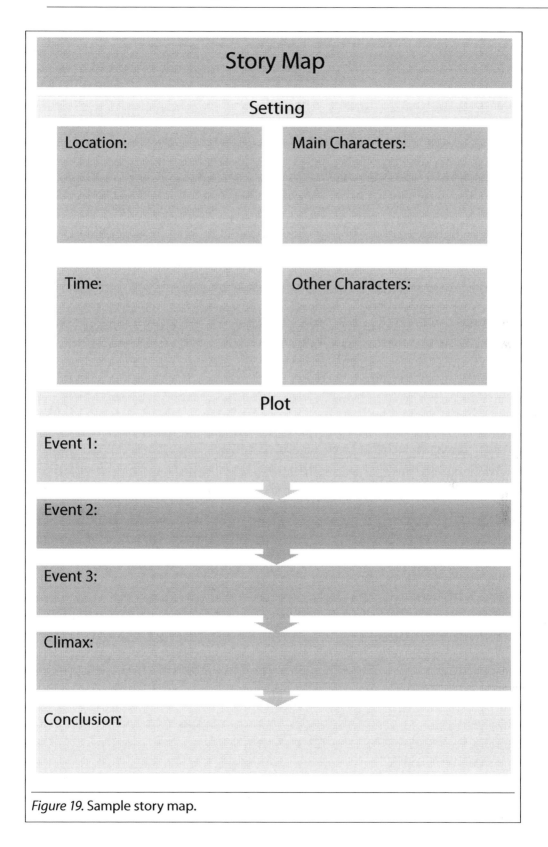

Figure 19. Sample story map.

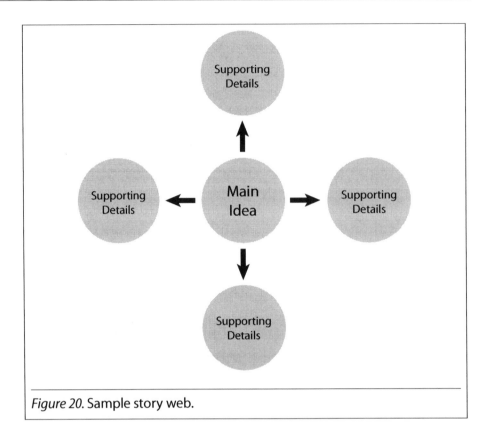

Figure 20. Sample story web.

very frustrated and bored with grade-level math. Math performance improves with compensatory strategies like emphasis on word problems, the use of calculators, and additional time for assignments (Hishinuma & Tadaki, 1996).

Strategies for Overcoming Math Difficulties

- Adapt the pace of instruction. Twice-exceptional learners need differentiated instruction that helps them develop the habits of mind of mathematicians. The pace of instruction must be at a level appropriate for the student:
  - The content should be differentiated to provide greater abstraction and complexity.
  - The process should emphasize mathematical concepts, higher level thinking, and the development of problem-solving skills rather than computation skills.
  - The problems should be open-ended with multiple solutions and address real-world scenarios.
- Provide opportunities for twice-exceptional learners to look for patterns, experiment to find solutions, and learn the mathematical language. Participation in Math Counts, Mathematical Olympiads, and American Junior and High School Mathematical Exams promotes mathematical thinking.

- Allow twice-exceptional learners to use calculators and computers to complete high-level mathematical problems.

- Assess mathematical skills and provide explicit instruction to help students develop skills in their areas of weakness.

- Provide support for specific weaknesses. For example, the sequential thinking required to solve some mathematical problems like long division and algebra can be a problem area for twice-exceptional learners.

- Encourage students to set personal goals and work to improve their fluency completing one-minute fluency speed drills on basic math addition, subtraction, multiplication, and division computations similar to the one-minute readings for fluency. Learning such math facts and recalling them is a problem area for twice-exceptional learners. Chart personal growth and celebrate attainment of goals.

SUMMARY

The academic achievement of twice-exceptional learners is characterized by inconsistent performance. Problems arise when teachers do not recognize that gifted learners can have disabilities and view the students as lazy, unmotivated, or defiant. The view that gifted students who do not complete assignments are irresponsible can result in a punitive approach when what these students need is empathy and encouragement. Early recognition of learning problems and appropriate interventions can prevent the development of social and emotional issues. Problems with fluency and automaticity of basic skills such as phonemic awareness, decoding skills, handwriting, and learning math facts are areas of deficit that require early intervention and explicit systematic instruction. This chapter discussed dyslexia, dysgraphia, and dyscalculia and provided specific interventions. When developing an intervention plan for twice-exceptional learners, it is important to include strategies for developing the student's potential as well as implement interventions in deficit areas. Excelling in their area of strength builds the resilience students need to overcome their disabilities.

Chapter 7

FOSTERING INTERPERSONAL RELATIONSHIPS

Twice-exceptional learners struggle with perceptions of being different and feelings of isolation (King, 2005; Nielsen & Higgins, 2005). Asynchronous development and discrepancies between academic and social abilities are contributing factors to poor peer relationships and academic problems (Brody & Mills, 1997). Advanced cognitive abilities can lead to social isolation when the student is not able to relate to his peers (Neihart, 1999). Along with other students with learning disabilities, twice-exceptional students have more social problems than their peers without disabilities. These problems include difficulty using appropriate social skills, generating solutions to social problems, and interpreting social cues (Stormont, Stebbins, & Holiday, 2001). Students with Asperger's syndrome or Nonverbal Learning Disorder cannot read nonverbal social clues. Instruction in social thinking that focuses on understanding how to interact with others; using appropriate body language, gestures, facial expressions, and physical proximity; and tone, pitch, and loudness of voice is helpful (Nielsen & Higgins,

2005). Learning how to think about others and to anticipate what people think about them is also very important (Winner, 2002).

Peer Relationships

Gifted students with disabilities are vulnerable to a number of social issues that can hamper their development. Possessing both the characteristics of gifted students and those of students with disabilities can make it difficult for twice-exceptional learners to fit in with either gifted students or students who have disabilities. It is important for twice-exceptional learners to develop positive relationships with children like themselves because this provides a basis for healthy peer relationships and promotes the development of self-confidence (Goerss, 2005). Research has demonstrated the importance of having the support of other gifted students in promoting achievement and reversing underachievement (Reis & McCoach, 2002). Social problems can diminish the full development of the student's potential and can lead to underachievement (Olenchak & Reis, 2002).

Normal social development is necessary for personal success. Gifted children can feel isolated when their asynchronous development causes them to be out of sync with age peers. Greg described it this way: "I guess it is the contrast. I had mental abilities back then that were ahead of the norm and the disconnect of not being able to relate to kids my own age that well." Twice-exceptional children find it difficult to relate with their age peers as well as with other gifted learners or age peers with disabilities. The disability intensifies the problems and further isolates these children. Cognitive development that is not in sync with social/emotional development can make students vulnerable socially. Gaining acceptance from other gifted students increases the self-esteem of twice-exceptional learners. Loneliness and social isolation is not the result of emotional problems, but the lack of suitable peers. When students are not able to establish relationships with peers, they are unable to complete a basic developmental task that could profoundly affect their future (Goerss, 2005).

Twice-exceptional learners particularly need support with social interactions when they are facing the challenges of adolescence (Cohen & Wills, 1985). Greg wanted more than anything else to just be normal and fit in with his peers. He commented:

> They know that you are different. I don't know how to explain it other than say that. People just realize that I am not normal, I'm not, I don't interact with people the way others do. I don't know how to explain it or if it is even real or some kind of paranoia or something. It seems like other people are so . . . [Greg paused and then continued.] It is so easy to kind of submerge their identity for the group. You know, in a lot of social situations that is important and if you don't do that, it kind of marks you as a leper.

Peer Bullying

Advanced cognitive abilities, poor social skills, and sensitivity left Greg vulnerable to peer bullying. Greg was bullied throughout elementary and middle school and he internalized their negative comments. He told me,

> It got to the point where I felt like other people were just going to be hassles for me. I didn't feel like interacting with them and for a long time I just didn't. I felt like social stuff was below me and I was going to ignore it. Which is all well and good when you are 8 but then you get to be 14, 15, 16 in high school and you realize those are important things. All of a suddenly you realize you are stuck with the abilities of someone much younger.

Gifted students sometimes change their identity to one that is more socially acceptable (Gross, 1998). Greg hated middle school because "social skills became more important, and I have always felt [behind] in my social growth." It was during this time that "Greg started to become more flat in his affect and really just pulled the hood over the head kind of thing," explained his mom. Greg camouflaged his gifted identity and adopted the behaviors of his peers in an attempt to become part of a popular group and according to his mom, "worked hard to get off the honor roll because he was teased for being a 'school boy.'" He did not want to be different from his peers. Greg commented:

> A lot of my speech patterns and stuff are just remnants of trying to act like I was of average intelligence as though that would allow me to blend in or something. But it just, I don't know, it doesn't. I guess it is like something that is hard for me to deal with. I have a lot of trouble with it. It is like the aloneness of it. I don't feel like I am always lonely. A lot of times I like being alone. I feel very isolated from the kind of contact that it seems like a lot of people take for granted.

Failure to bond with peers meant Greg was unable to experience normal social development. A desire for friends became his primary focus and football enabled him to join the popular kids. "I was trying to learn all the social stuff," he said. Wild parties, excessive drinking, and drugs took over his life as he worked to improve his social skills. Soon Greg was in trouble, not because he did not know right from wrong, but because he chose to ignore it to achieve peer acceptance. The consequences of his actions were devastating and he attempted suicide and later spent time in a residential substance abuse treatment center and a detention center. Greg commented, "My choices got me in trouble in high school. It is easy to say I was hanging out with the cool kids, but that doesn't absolve you. I knew what was right and wrong, I just chose to ignore it. I can't really blame anyone else for that."

Asynchronous development means students with advanced cognitive and academic abilities may have less developed social skills. The asynchrony in their development makes them feel different from their peers and, particularly in a school with an anti-intellectual climate, can leave them vulnerable to peer bullying. Greg tried to submerge his gifted identity in order to gain acceptance by his peers, but he continued to feel isolated. Implementing options for grade acceleration would have resulted in a curriculum that was more challenging and grade-level peers who were more similar in their cognitive and academic abilities.

Many twice-exceptional learners need assistance in developing the communication and collaboration skills needed to relate effectively with others. They may have advanced verbal skills, but not know how to communicate. Some twice-exceptional learners do not understand nonverbal communication skills such as facial expressions, gestures, tone of voice, posture, and personal space. Small-group instruction and targeted interventions where students view movie clips without sound and interpret the nonverbal clues can be effective in teaching these skills.

Another important skill is to learn how to identify the perspectives and intensions of others. For example, Spencer was active in his high school computer club when several members of the group asked him to change their grades. He knew it wasn't right but he wanted their friendship and they praised his computer skills, which made him feel accepted. When the school discovered the changed grades and confronted the students, they implicated Spencer. The school suspended Spencer, and he felt betrayed by his so-called friends. He subsequently attempted suicide and spent the rest of the semester in a treatment center.

Strategies to Improve Peer Relationships

- Create a safe environment. Schools and classroom environments must foster respect for individuals and individual differences. Do not allow students to treat each other with disrespect. Strive to develop empathetic feeling among students.

- Guard students against bullying and provide training on bullying. It is the teachers' and administrators' responsibilities to make sure students are not bullied in school. Students who are bullied are victims and they need counseling and help with developing skills that will make them less vulnerable to bullying. Ask the school counselor to come into your class and talk to students about bullying and help them understand the following points:

  - They do not need to be a victim of bullying. Teach them how to avoid situations where they could be bullied and provide a safe place students can go to escape bullying.

  - The bully does not control their life. Teach students to take control by standing tall, making eye contact with the person who is bullying them, and telling the bully to stop.

- Students who are bullied often continue to bully themselves with negative self-talk after a bullying incident. Help them rebuild their self-confidence by thinking about their positive traits and accomplishments and focusing on achieving personal goals and taking control of their life.

- Identify students who are at risk and need help with interpersonal relationships by observing students interacting with others. Include those students in supervised friendship groups where they can develop skills.

- Group and regroup students flexibly according to interest, ability, strengths, or learning styles. Provide opportunities for students to work with peers who have similar interests, ability, strengths, or learning styles.

- Brainstorm a list of skills that are important in developing and maintaining friendships with the whole class. These are a few of the skills students need to develop:
  - how to approach others and introduce yourself,
  - asking to join a group to play a game,
  - sharing and waiting your turn,
  - beginning and sharing a conversation with others, and
  - giving compliments and saying thank you.

- Use discussions of literature to increase students' understanding, to discuss problems, to foster honest self-appraisal, or to chart a course of action. A facilitator guides individual students or a group of students in discussions to interpret, apply, analyze, synthesize, and evaluate the information (Aiex, 1993). Figure 21 provides a list of books that can be used as bibliotherapy with twice-exceptional students.

- Teach friendship skills, including how to begin a conversation, asking someone to play, sharing, playing a game, or waiting turns.

- Practice social skills in a safe structured environment where students can practice and learn friendship skills. Invite children with similar interests to play or work together on a project and supervise their interactions.

- Model how to greet others, share a conversation, listen carefully, ask someone for help, offer help, say "thank you," give a compliment, ask a favor, and apologize.

- Have students reflect on their social skills. Practicing social skills learned and reflecting on what happened is an important element of metacognitive learning. After teaching a skill, ask students to practice the skill for a week and reflect on the results using the weekly review form in Figure 22.

Picture Books

How to Be a Friend by Marc Brown

The Care and Keeping of Friends by Nadine Bernard Westcott

Bullies Are a Pain in the Brain by Trevor Romain

We Are Best Friends by Aliki

Join In and Play by Cheri J. Meiners

How to Lose All Your Friends by Nancy Carlson

Words Are Not for Hurting by Elizabeth Verdick

No Ordinary Olive by Roberta Baker

Stand Tall, Molly Lou Melon by Patty Lovell

Odd Velvet by Mary E. Whitcomb

Wemberly Worried by Kevin Henkes

Middle Grades/Young Adult Books

Alice, I Think by Susan Juby

Deep by Susanna Vance

Green Thumb by Rob Thomas

Someday Angeline by Louis Sachar

You Don't Know Me by David Klass

A Solitary Blue by Cynthia Voigt

Ella Enchanted by Gail Carson Levine

Joey Pigza Swallowed the Key by Jack Gantos

Millicent Min, Girl Genius by Lisa Yee

The Report Card by Andrew Clements

The Two Princesses of Bamarre by Gail Carson Levine

Figure 21. Books for bibliotherapy with twice-exceptional students.

Weekly Review	
This week I will practice:	
Place a tally mark in the box at the right every time you practice the skill.	
As a result of my hard work: • I was successful in using the skill. • I need more practice.	
I learned . . .	
Next time I will . . .	

Figure 22. Social skills reflection form.

RELATIONSHIPS WITH TEACHERS

The inconsistent academic performance of twice-exceptional students can have a negative influence on their relationships with teachers. Although these students demonstrate superior abilities in problem solving, abstract thinking, and creativity, their achievement may be more reflective of a student with disabilities. Their advanced verbal skills raise teachers' expectations. When the twice-exceptional learner fails to turn in assignments, teachers tend to think they are not acting responsible or investing enough effort. Many twice-exceptional learners lack organizational and time management skills necessary for managing multiple assignments. They may avoid assignments in areas related to their disability. Teachers do not understand the inconsistent academic achievement of twice-exceptional learners, nor do they understand that these students can have both strengths and deficits in the same academic area. For instance, a child may have strengths in mathematical problem solving along with a weakness in memorizing math facts. Christina could solve difficult mathematical story problems, but her scores on the timed multiplication fact tests were dismal. Learning the sequential steps needed to solve long division problems was difficult even though she knew the correct answer. She told me, "I know the answer to this problem, but the steps do not make sense to me." She eventually made sense of the process, but the experience was frustrating.

Unfortunately, teachers sometimes do not realize a disability is affecting the academic achievement of twice-exceptional learners. All too often, their underachievement is attributed to lack of motivation or laziness (Silverman, 1989; Waldron et al., 1987; Whitmore, 1980). These negative attributions can dramatically influence the way teachers respond to children. Teachers are less empathetic toward students they believe are acting irresponsible or simply not trying. Instead of the encouraging response teachers should provide for struggling students, twice-exceptional students sometimes receive a more punitive response. Having exceptional abilities and disabilities that interfere with learning, when one or both of the conditions are unrecognized, delays appropriate diagnosis and programming. The extreme frustration these students experience when their giftedness and disability are not recognized, can lead to behavior problems and the focus on interventions moves to behavior management. This delay can result in social and emotional consequences that can be quite debilitating (Baum et al., 1991; Brody & Mills, 1997; Durden & Tangherlini, 1993; Fox, Brody, & Tobin, 1983; Whitmore, 1980).

Research by Trail (2008) found that the role of teachers in the education of twice-exceptional learners should not be underestimated. According to Greg, teachers made the difference: "There were certain teachers who really made it fun to learn. They were engaging and didn't treat kids as their job. They treated teaching like it was something they wanted to be doing." He preferred teachers who cared about learning and were personally interested in their students. Greg felt it was important for teachers to be approachable and available to talk with students outside of class. Todd also thrived when his teachers were flexible and provided challenging learning opportunities. Conversely, he was often at odds with teachers who were inflexible and regimented. Teachers who demanded students do things their way brought out a defiant attitude in both boys. Flexibility is important for twice-exceptional learners. They need teachers who allow students to vary assignments so they can use their strengths and preferred cognitive styles to process information and to demonstrate their knowledge.

Todd was very critical of his fourth- and fifth-grade teachers for being so rigid and set in what they wanted him to do. "They were not interested at all in me doing anything other than what everyone else was doing." Todd continued, "I just felt it wasn't a constructive place for me to be. I don't think I learned nearly as much and I didn't enjoy learning nearly as much as I did when I was in sixth grade." Fortunately, his sixth-grade teacher was more flexible and Todd developed a good relationship with this teacher. On the other hand, Greg dropped out of high school when he encountered an inflexible math teacher. He had this to say about his interaction with this teacher:

> I really liked math when I was a kid and then in high school, I really started disliking it largely because you were forced to write out steps. I shouldn't have to write out 7 x 2 = 14 in a high school level class. That is just my opinion. For me to be docked points for not doing it really got under my skin. I don't like the teachers that say there is only one way to do a problem, "my way." Your own way doesn't matter even if you get the right answer because you needed to do it "my way." It really drove me wild in math; teachers who would take points off for doing it in less steps blows my mind. If the end result is correct, I don't think it should really matter how you got it. If I write down on my test I know this because God told me the answer in my ear, it shouldn't matter as long as the answer is correct. I just remember that semester it got to a point, it was a kind of a breaking point for me. I felt as if school was a waste of my time. I'm sitting here and I have to jump through hoops for some lady who's just completely incompetent.

It is important that teachers provide challenging learning opportunities and support their students when they struggle to learn. Todd said, "If a teacher I like asked me to do something, even if I don't feel inclined to do it, I will do it because I recognize they are [sic] a good teacher and they probably know what they are [sic] doing." Todd was willing to persevere and practice monotonous tasks to improve his skills when he respected the teacher and the teacher acknowledged his strengths (Trail, 2008).

Strategies to Improve Relationships Between Teachers and Students

- Connect with your students and let them know that you really care about them. When there is a teacher/student connection, students are more willing to work hard and complete assignments so as not to disappoint their teacher.

- Recognize when a gifted student is not achieving commensurate with his ability and make a referral to determine if the student has a hidden disability.

- Support and encourage twice-exceptional learners as they work to develop skills in areas related to their disability.

- Discussion activities engage twice-exceptional students. Brainstorming teacher-pleasing skills like the following may be effective in helping twice-exceptional learners understand why these things are important.
  - listening, following instructions;
  - asking for help, waiting for help, saying "thank you";
  - bringing materials to class, completing assignments;
  - working independently, working in a group;
  - ignoring distractions, not disturbing others; and
  - accepting criticism, handling frustration, and finding self-control.

- Consult your gifted education and/or special education specialist for suggestions. Refer the student for additional assessments to determine if a disability may be the cause of the underachievement.

- Differentiate the curriculum so students are challenged at the level that is appropriate for them. If the challenge level is too high, students are frustrated and if it is too low, students become bored.

- Be flexible and allow students to process information using their preferred learning and thinking styles. Provide choice in assignments so they are able to use their strengths to demonstrate what they know.

- Celebrate successes and encourage students to persist through the frustration to achieve academic success.

FAMILY DYNAMICS

Family support, attachment, and approval (Sheeber, Davis, Leve, Hops, & Tildesley, 2007) are of prime importance in the development of twice-exceptional learners. High levels of family cohesion and close family relations result in more positive outcomes (Trail, 2008). Twice-exceptional learners can be empowered to overcome their disabilities by their families. Conversely, through their interactions within their family, twice-exceptional students can develop learned helplessness. It is difficult for parents to watch their children struggle, and some parents will rush in to rescue their children from failure, but this can lead to negative consequences that decrease the children's self-esteem. It sends a clear message to the children, that their parents do not feel they are capable of meeting the challenges of school without their help. Conversely, self-esteem increases when the children learn to deal with their disability and the frustrations they encounter in school. When twice-exceptional children learn to solve their problems and successfully overcome the challenges, they gain control over their lives, which helps them to mature and become self-sufficient.

Focus on Fixing

Well-intentioned parents become enablers when they focus on fixing and rescuing their child with disabilities. Parents can become so focused on fixing a child that some take their child from one specialist to the next trying to find someone who will change the child. These parents tend to become enablers. The process of enabling can begin quite innocently when a parent steps in to help a child who has procrastinated and put off completing an assignment until the night before it is due. Parents can easily take over the responsibility of the project, sending a message to the child that he is not capable. The parent takes away the opportunity for the child to experience the natural consequences of his behavior. Instead of learning from mistakes, the child becomes increasingly dependent on the parent. The child needs increasing amounts of help and soon the parent is doing more of the work than the child. The more help the parent gives, the less capable the child feels and his self-esteem decreases. Self-esteem increases when a child accomplishes something he believes to be difficult (Rimm, 1989), such as learning to solve his own problems.

Empowering Parents

Empowering parents see their children as capable of solving their own problems. They focus their attention on finding opportunities for their children to develop potential. The disability is viewed as an inconvenience and they help their children learn compensatory strategies. These parents believe they are responsible for guiding their children toward developing the skills they need to become independent and personally responsible. When problems arise, the parents help their children figure out options and available resources. These parents know the importance of being a role model for their children. They actively teach their children how to make decisions and solve their problems. These parents know their young children will not always make the perfect decisions, but will learn valuable lessons when the natural consequences are minimal. Children feel empowered when they successfully solve problems on their own. These positive experiences help them grow and mature. Of course, parents need to intervene if the child is in crisis or if a wrong decision could result in serious consequences. Empowering parents help their children to grow as individuals, gain independence, and become personally responsible.

Strategies to Empower Children
- Focus on what the children can do rather than the things they cannot do.
- Instead of trying to fix your children, search for opportunities where your children can develop their strengths and interests.
- Encourage your children to participate in extracurricular school activities and community-based programs. They will have fun learning and meet children who have similar interests.
- Model behaviors that will help your children learn how to make friends and get along with teachers. Children learn more from what you do than what you say.
- Recognize that it is important for your children to have friends and do what you can to involve your children in activities where they can meet other children.
- Create a home environment where your children will be comfortable inviting friends over to play. Have tasty and healthy treats available as well as engaging games and activities so their friends will want to visit.
- Work collaboratively with the school to design a plan of interventions to be implemented at both home and school.

AFFILIATION VERSES ISOLATION

Twice-exceptional learners who are involved in extracurricular activities in school are more likely to stay in school and graduate. Participation in extracurricular activities (Nettle, Mucherah, & Jones, 2000) and having a talent or hobby that was valued by peers promoted resiliency and increased social support from peers (Cauce, Felner, & Primavera, 1982). Todd's involvement in Destination Imagination gave him a chance to develop his creative ability and an opportunity to work with peers who shared his interests. Over the years, he developed deep friendships and had lots of fun. Also, through involvement in a music program, Todd discovered his love of music. He gained the respect of his peers as section leader and he developed his leadership skills. When Greg became disillusioned with school, he dropped out of a talent search program. At that point, he did not want to be viewed as different; instead he just wanted to blend in with his peers. Participation in this activity would have given him a chance to develop his strengths and to grow friendships with other gifted children.

Introverts and extroverts react very differently to stressful experiences. Research has found variations in brain function rather than experiences account

Extroverts	• People oriented • Perfer to work in groups • Are energized by people and group work • Active learners
Introverts	• Task oriented • Prefer to work alone • Group work drains personal energy and they need time alone to regain strength • Reflective learners

Figure 23. Qualities of extroverts and introverts.

for differences between extroversion and introversion. PET scans revealed that introverts had more activity in the frontal lobes and anterior or thalamus. These areas are responsible for problem solving and planning. Introverts are quiet, inwardly focused, and reclusive. The cingulated gyrus, temporal lobes, and posterior thalamus were more active in extroverts. These areas are involved in sensory processing for listening or watching. Extroverts are gregarious, socially active, and sensation seeking. Being around others is personally energizing for extroverts. On the other hand, group activities drain introverts. Introverts need time alone to reenergize. Figure 23 illustrates the characteristics of introverts and extroverts.

The students' decision to participation in extracurricular activities may be influenced by their personality styles. You probably will not be surprised to learn that Todd is an extrovert and Greg is an introvert. When Todd was stressed, he had a large group of friends he could turn to for support. The group was considered the unpopular group, but it was larger than the popular group. Todd was accepted in this group for who he was. On the other hand, Greg escaped into solitude to reflect during times of stress. When he broke up with his girlfriend, he stopped going to class and to work. He spent time alone in his apartment. He needed help in learning more productive coping strategies he could use during times of stress. It is not important how many activities students are engaged in or how many friends they have. Involvement in one activity and having one or two close friends may be all a student needs. It is just important that the student does not feel alienated in the school environment or among classmates.

Strategies to Keep Students Engaged in School

- Encourage students to participate in extracurricular or community activities. Seek activities related to the students' interests where they can develop their strengths and make friends with students who have similar interests.

- Make sure your school provides a variety of activities and opportunities for introverted students to participate in a small intimate group and larger group activities for extroverted students.

- Mentorships and apprenticeships can be invaluable experiences for twice-exceptional learners. Look for mentors with similar interests who can share how they overcame their disabilities to become successful. An apprenticeship gives students the opportunity to gain work experience in a field they are interested in pursuing. A career goal may be the key to keeping students focused on graduating so they can attend college and pursue their chosen career.

ADVOCACY

Advocating for twice-exceptional learners can be extremely difficult. Parents' and teachers' attempts to advocate can be met with fierce resistance. One of the main reasons for this is the fact that many educators do not understand or recognize the diverse needs of twice-exceptional learners. Well-intentioned teachers can focus on what the student is not doing. They tend to perceive a gifted student who does not complete assignments as capable but lazy, unmotivated, or defiant. Twice-exceptional children often complain they are bored in school, but teachers, in turn, have many examples of incomplete assignments they can share to refute the children's claims. Some teachers are not aware how emotionally fragile twice-exceptional students can be. These students may be able to keep their emotions hidden while at school, but their behavior at home makes it very clear that something is seriously wrong. Do not dismiss parents' concerns. Recognize that it is frustrating for teachers, parents, and students when they are unable to achieve to others' or their own expectations. Many parents of twice-exceptional learners are gifted adults who have disabilities. They may have experienced the same problems in school and want to make sure their children have a better experience.

Strategies for Advocating for Twice-Exceptional Learners

- Review facts and assessment data. Gain a clear understanding of the academic, social, and emotional issues that are influencing academic achievement.

- Understand the students' perspective. Effective advocates provide information that will help others understand the students. It can be difficult to gain students' confidence to learn their perspective. Use a nonjudgmental demeanor and try to make one-to-one connection at eye level. You can also do this using the following methods:
  - Paraphrase or rephrase and repeat back what children tell you. It confirms to them that you are listening to what they are saying.
  - Ask open-ended questions: What happened? What happened before this? What did you want to happen? How did you feel? What was the other person doing? How did he or she feel?
  - Following a question with a question helps you and the children get a clearer understanding of the problem and their feelings.

- Interview parents and teachers. Using open-ended questions can help you probe for meaning. Identify the problem from the point of view of each participant and learn as much as you can about events leading to the underachievement.

- Avoid the blame game. Communicate your concerns as clearly as possible without blame. Nothing is accomplished by blaming others except bad feelings. Act as a role model for the student as you advocate for his or her best interests.

- Clearly identify the problem and work collaboratively in the problem-solving process. Keep the focus on the student's academic, social, and emotional needs. Follow the steps of collaborative problem solving in Chapter 2.

SELF-ADVOCACY

Twice-exceptional learners try to hide their disabilities from peers and teachers because they want others to recognize their gifted potential rather than their disability. They impose unrealistic expectations on themselves and do not ask for help because they believe that they should be able to solve their own problems. It is extremely important for them to learn that asking for help is not a sign of weakness. Teachers have to recognize how difficult it is for twice-exceptional learners to ask for help and they need to listen to what they have to say. Twice-exceptional learners need help in developing self-advocacy skills so they can advocate for themselves.

Strategies to Help Students Become Self-Advocates

- Assist students in understanding their strengths, weaknesses, and learning styles. They can provide valuable insights into strategies that will help them to be successful in school. Involve students in the problem-solving process and give them a voice in telling others what they need to be successful in school.

- Help students develop the communication skills they need to be able to advocate for themselves. Role-play how to approach a teacher to schedule a meeting and then practice the meeting.

- Brainstorm teacher-pleasing skills and coach the student in developing skills like the following:
  - Arrive at class on time and bring the required materials to class.
  - Follow instructions and complete assignments in a timely manner.
  - Ask for help when you do not understand expectations.
  - Raise your hand when you want to answer a question or ask for help.
  - Do not be overly sensitive to criticism because your teacher is trying to guide you in becoming a more successful student.
  - Work collaboratively in a group, listen to what the other students have to say, and compromise when necessary.
  - Learn how to handle frustration, demonstrate self-control, and manage your own behavior.

SUMMARY

Interpersonal relationships can be a problem for twice-exceptional students with asynchronous development, especially those with Asperger's syndrome or Nonverbal Learning Disorder. These students can lag behind classmates in developing the interpersonal skills needed to function effectively in social groups. They may have a difficult time interpreting social cues and generating solutions to social problems (Stormont et al., 2001). Twice-exceptional learners can become targets of peer bullying. Schools must assume responsibility for not allowing bullying and for providing a safe environment to meet the academic, social, and emotional needs of their students. Students who are not able to develop normal interpersonal relationships with peers need supervised friendship groups where they can learn social skills and practice interacting with peers. These twice-exceptional learners may need help developing teacher-pleasing skills and positive relationships with their teachers. Learning skills of self-advocacy will help to alleviate some of their problems with teachers. Frustrated parents may enable their children instead of empowering them to deal with their asynchronous development and disabilities. The problem-solving team or social worker may need to provide guidance for parents so they can develop skills to empower their children.

Involvement in extracurricular and community activities gives students a chance to develop friendships with others who have similar interests. Mentorships and apprenticeships can be beneficial for twice-exceptional learners. Developing a relationship with a successful adult who has overcome a disability would be beneficial. An apprenticeship may motivate students to achieve better grades so they can pursue their career goals. Improving interpersonal relationships increases resilience and has a positive influence on achievement.

Chapter 8

PROMOTING INTRAPERSONAL UNDERSTANDING

Disabilities increase the social and emotional vulnerability of twice-exceptional learners. They are more prone to underachievement, low self-esteem, emotional problems, and higher dropout rates than their peers (Spekman et al., 1993). The literature describes characteristics of poor self-concept, reduced self-efficacy, anxiety, hypersensitivity, elevated levels of frustration, and self-criticism (Baum et al., 1991; Higgins & Nielsen, 1999; Olenchak, 1994; Waldron et al., 1987; Whitmore, 1980). Many twice-exceptional students have painful memories of negative school situations when they encountered repeated punishment for not completing work on time (Olenchak & Reis, 2002). Dysfunctional perfectionism, intensity of emotions (Silverman, 1989), oversensitivity, low self-esteem, and intense frustration with difficult tasks negatively influence these students' achievement. This chapter discusses the emotional issues that twice-exceptional learners deal with as they try to make sense of discrepancies in their ability. Interventions are designed to help students develop intrapersonal understanding so they can deal with the emotional issues that can negatively influence their achievement and satisfaction with life.

CONFUSION AND ANXIETY

Twice-exceptional learners experience extreme frustration trying to deal with both exceptionalities. The unevenness of abilities within these learners contributes to their vulnerability. Advanced vocabulary and communication skills increases the expectations of parents and teachers. It is difficult for parents and educators to understand why a verbally precocious student has difficulty writing his or her ideas on a piece of paper. Expectations that gifted students have similar abilities within the same content area can result in the assumption that the student is not putting forward a reasonable amount of effort. Lack of achievement in gifted students often is perceived as lack of effort. Often these students have been told to "shape up" and "work harder" by teachers who were aware of their advanced verbal abilities and thought the students were lazy (Olenchak & Reis, 2002). The inconsistent messages they receive from teachers, parents, and peers leads twice-exceptional learners to question their abilities.

As twice-exceptional learners progress through the grades, it becomes more difficult for them to compensate for their disabilities. Delays in the identification of their gifted potential and/or disabilities can result in the development of social and emotional problems. Research indicates that gifted students with disabilities struggle with unrealistic expectations (Baum et al., 1991). It can be confusing for gifted students to understand and deal with discrepancies in their abilities (King, 2005). Similar to other gifted learners, they hold high expectations for themselves and for others. However, achieving these expectations can be difficult for students with deficits in cognitive processing, executive functioning, and academic skills.

Unfortunately, the confusion that results from being gifted and having a disability can result in feelings of frustration, depression, low self-esteem, fear of failure, helplessness, and a heightened sense of inefficacy (Baum et al., 1991). These gifted learners begin to question their abilities when they fail to meet their own expectations or the expectations of others. For many twice-exceptional learners school was easy in the early elementary years, but as they progressed through the grades, it became much more difficult to maintain high grades. The discrepancies in their abilities can cause them to feel like an imposter. They need to understand that gifted individuals do at times flounder and need help from others to achieve their goals. As Albert Einstein's sister reported, he

> never was much good at the "easy" part of mathematics. To shine, he had
> to move on to the "hard" part. In adult life his mathematical intuition
> was recognised as extraordinary and he could handle deftly the most dif-

ficult of tensor calculus, but it appears that arithmetic calculation continued to be an area of comparative weakness. ("Dyslexia—Einstein," n.d., para. 8)

High expectations of the students, their teachers, and their parents, combined with delays in identifying learning disabilities, can contribute to the development of emotional issues.

Perfectionism and Procrastination

Gifted students tend to have heightened expectations and high standards for achievement that are not always realistic (Coleman, 2001; Vespi & Yewchuk, 1992). Learning to strive for personal excellence is an important element in developing gifted potential. Many gifted students are able to achieve academic success with little effort in their elementary years. As a result, these students develop the unrealistic expectation that school will always be easy. Brandon was able to achieve good grades in elementary school even though he had an undiagnosed disability. However, in middle school he was no longer able to compensate for his disability. He became increasingly frustrated with school and had a difficult time understanding why it had become so hard. After receiving a failing grade on a homework assignment for not following directions, he did not hand in a single assignment. His mother, an assistant principal, was surprised to learn he had not handed in these assignments because she had checked each one and knew he had completed them. When asked why he had not handed in the completed assignments, Brandon replied that he was afraid of getting another F. In his mind, it was better to not hand the homework and get a 0 then to risk getting an F. His perfectionism had become dysfunctional, and he was experiencing paralyzing anxiety.

Dysfunctional perfectionism can result when students set unrealistic goals (Olenchak, 1994). For the dysfunctional perfectionist, every new project is a step on the road to possible failure and any performance short of spectacular is viewed as failure (Adderholdt-Elliott, 1987). Fear of failure can lead to procrastination, frustration, off-task behaviors, and defensive behaviors (Beckley, 1998) to disguise students' feelings of low self-esteem and diminished academic self-efficacy. Students with dysfunctional perfectionism often believe that if they will not get an A then they do not want to risk failure. For the perfectionist, mistakes are not seen as a part of the learning process.

Twice-exceptional students can be caught in a cycle of perfectionism, avoidance, and procrastination. Chronic stress caused internally by perfectionism or externally from a stressful environment can impair a student's short- and long-term memory (Jacobs & Nadel, 1985). Their ability to sort out what is important and what is not is compromised (Gazzaniga, 1988). Stressful environments can trigger chemical imbalances in the brain, and these imbalances can result in impulsive, aggressive behavior (Jensen, 1998). The typical school environment can be very stressful for the twice-exceptional learner who is trying to deal with perfectionism and unrealistic expectations. It is important for these students to understand the role that mistakes play in the learning process. Helping students learn coping strategies to deal with the challenges and disappointments in their life is important.

Greg particularly has struggled with unrealistic expectations and dysfunctional perfectionism. When I asked Greg what his biggest challenge was he didn't have to stop to think before he quickly replied:

> Myself mostly, I guess. I am very hard on myself. Everyone tells me that, I just don't know what to do about it. I realize a lot of my thoughts are irrational yet somehow they seem rational in my head and it is hard not to think them. The main thing is perfectionism. It is impossible to be perfect.

Greg also related to the notion that twice-exceptional students' standards are not always realistic: "Yea, that is what I have been told, I am unrealistic, I hold standards that aren't really practical. It is kind of a 'setting myself up to fail' situation." He continued, "If it's not 100%, then it's pointless. That is one of those stupid things. I feel like if it is not a complete success, it is a failure." I told him I had noticed that for many twice-exceptional students everything is either black or white. He said, "It is hard for me to see the shades of gray that a lot of people do. Perfectionism has always been the trouble."

Twice-exceptional students can develop many creative ways to avoid failure (Coleman, 1992). Avoidance, procrastination, distancing, and learned helplessness are negative coping strategies. Students can take on the persona of a rebel who is too smart to complete the assignment that is too boring or too stupid. They can become the class clown, because it was better to be asked to leave the class for clowning around than to fail. One of my students assumed the role of teacher assistant, helping all of the other students with their projects to avoid taking responsibility for his own project. Perfectionists have to learn that mistakes are part of the learning process. It is important to help students develop positive coping strategies such as accepting responsibility for their actions instead of blaming others. Coping is defined as developing behaviors to manage specific external and/or internal demands that exceed the resources of that person (Folkman & Lazarus, 1988). Students with learning problems need to be systematically taught coping strategies (Coleman, 1992). Teachers should focus attention on helping students learn skills to manage stressful situations. This includes skills to appraise the positive and negative aspects of their work and to develop a problem-solving strategy to overcome any problems.

Effort or Ability

Research by Reis and McCoach (2002) found that underachieving students attributed success to luck and failure to lack of ability. Twice-exceptional learners tend to fall into this group because they can achieve in their area of strength with little effort yet it is difficult for them to deal with the frustration they feel when they struggle. Achieving students believed success was achieved through effort and failure was attributed to lack of effort.

Greg thought of his advanced academic abilities as a "born thing." It was not something he worked to achieve. He was able to get good grades without investing effort. He commented, "I never learned the discipline to put the right effort in." In order for students to develop their full potential, they must learn to strive for their personal best and to invest the necessary effort to develop their potential. Teachers can assist students in making the connection between effort and achievement by complimenting them on their effort instead of ability. Provide learning opportunities where students are compelled to work to achieve their personal best. Relating success to personal growth rather than comparing students' work to that of their peers will compel students to continue to strive to achieve their personal best.

A research study found that students who were complimented on their effort were more likely to select challenging projects when given a choice, while students who were given compliments on their ability chose an easy project where they knew they could be successful (Schunk, 1984). It is much healthier to view giftedness as a talent that must be developed through hard work (Dweck, 1986). Consistently challenging curriculum is important for gifted learners because it helps them to develop good study habits and the perseverance necessary to be successful when the curriculum became more complex in the upper grades (Davis & Rimm, 2004). Students who learn that they can be successful if they put forth a reasonable amount of effort will learn to persist through the difficult times. Those who learn to equate success with effort will become achievers while those who attribute success to luck and failure to lack of ability will become underachievers. Teachers can help their students make the connection between hard work and success by praising their efforts, not their ability.

Strategies to Promote Intrapersonal Understanding in the Classroom
- Provide a safe climate in your classroom that values diversity and individual differences. Afford opportunities for students to learn about their strengths, weaknesses, and learning styles. Help students to understand that we all have weaknesses.

- Realize that some very bright twice-exceptional learners fear failure. Differentiate curriculum and instruction to provide challenge in the students' areas of strength and support in their areas of weakness. Make sure the students can successfully complete the tasks you assign and support them in their efforts to succeed.

- Focus on the students' strengths and developing their potential. Only after students have had an opportunity to develop their strengths and experience success will they be more willing to work on their weaknesses.

- Do not minimize the frustration students feel. Help them to understand that mistakes are part of the learning process.

- When you make a mistake, use it as a teaching opportunity to model mistakes as an important part of learning. Let the students know you have to risk failure in order to grow.

- Praise students' efforts, not their abilities. Support students in their academic efforts to achieve success.

UNDERSTANDING AND ACCEPTANCE

Research by Goerss (2005) found that both personal and academic success was more dependent on social and emotional development than curriculum. Twice-exceptional learners are at greater risk for social and emotional problems because of their dual exceptionalities. Personal awareness, understanding, and acceptance are essential for positive growth (Betts, 1985). Begin at an early age to assist students in developing a feeling vocabulary that can be used to express how they feel. In a brainstorming activity, develop a list of feeling words to cover as many different emotions as possible. Post these feeling words around the room. When you discuss stories in class, talk about how the characters feel and why they feel that way. Ask students to identify their own feelings on a scale of 1 to 10 and ask several of them to describe briefly why they feel the way they do. This activity will increase students' awareness of others feelings and promote the development of empathy for others.

Learning style inventories, multiple intelligence inventories, and interest surveys can help students identify their strengths and interests and enhance their understanding of how they learn. Many of these inventories are available online. There are many inventories to choose from and each addresses different concepts. Use several different ones and keep in mind that it is the conversations you have with students about the inventories that are important. You want students to come away from these conversations understanding that everyone has different interests, strengths, and weaknesses. The diversity of the group brings multiple perspectives and increases the chance to solve problems and make new discoveries. Group students so that they can use their strength in contributing to the group process. When students understand how they learn, they can become more efficient learners (Betts, 1991; Betts & Kercher, 1999).

Famous People With Disabilities

Studying famous people with disabilities helps twice-exceptional learners to realize they can be successful even though they have a disability. The entire class could benefit from studying famous people. Carefully guide twice-exceptional learners in selecting a famous person with a disability similar to theirs, but do not tell them about the famous person's disability. It is better if the students discover their disabilities through their own research. There are many websites that lists famous people with disabilities. Some of these identify the people according to specific disabilities. In Figure 24, I have identified just a few famous people according to their area of disability to get you started.

As students compare their characteristics to those of famous people, they begin to realize they have similar characteristics. Knowing that famous people had disabilities and struggled in school, but were able to become successful in later life and influence society in positive ways is very powerful. Discuss how these famous people were able to overcome their disabilities. Emphasize the important role of persistence and not giving up despite repeated failure. Small-group discussions after reading the biographies will help twice-exceptional learners to gain better insights into their feelings. Ask students to follow these steps in their study of a famous person:

1. *Select a famous person to study*: Encourage students to study a famous person who has interests similar to theirs. Decorate the room with pictures and quotes from famous people. Provide books, videos, and other resources available to address a variety of learning styles and ability levels.

2. *Brainstorm characteristics of famous people*: After students have time to learn about their famous person, brainstorm a list of characteristics of famous people.

3. *Identify the characteristics of your famous person*: Ask students to identify the characteristics of their famous person, including his or her strengths and weaknesses. The form in Figure 25 will be helpful for this task.

4. *Identify your own characteristics*: Recognize that this will be difficult for many students especially if they have low self-esteem.

5. *Compare and contrast characteristics*: Next, ask the students to identify characteristics that they share with the famous person studied.

Famous People With Disabilities		
Disability	Famous Person	Field of Emminance
Autism/Asperger's Syndrome	Tim Page Dawn Prince-Hughes Temple Grandin	Pulitzer Prize, Critic, Author Anthropologist, Ethologist College Professor, Author
ADHD	Richard Branson Robin Williams Michael Phelps	Entrepreneur Actor Olympic Swimmer
Blindness/Visual Impairment	Hellen Keller Louis Braille Steve Wonder Andrea Bocelli	Speaker, Author Inventor Singer, Songwritter Singer, Muscian
Communicative Disorders	Charles Darwin Wiston Churchill Lewis Carroll Bruce Willis	Naturalist Prime Minister Author Actor
Deafness/Hard of Hearing	Thomas Edison Marlee Matlin	Inventor Actress
Dyslexia	Albert Einstein Hans Christian Andersen Henry Winkler Tom Cruise	Mathematician, Physicist Author Actor, Author Actor
Learning Disabilities	Alexander Graham Bell Walt Disney George Patton	Inventor Producer, Entrepreneur Army General
Mood Disorder/Bipolar	Abraham Lincoln Mike Wallace Patty Duke	U.S. President Journalist Actress
Physical Disabilities	Stephen Hawking Franklin Roosevelt	Physics, Author U.S. President

Figure 24. Famous people with disabilities.

Compare Characteristics

Famous person's characteristics:	My characteristics:
•	•
•	•
•	•
•	•
•	•
•	•
•	•

We are similar in the following ways:

•

•

•

•

•

•

We are different in the following ways:

•

•

•

•

•

•

What I learned from this activity:

Figure 25. Form to help students identify the characteristics of famous people with disabilities.

The following strategies will help students to develop personal understanding and learn to be more accepting of their strengths and challenges:

- Assist students in developing a vocabulary of feeling words they can use to describe how they feel. Brainstorm a list of feeling words and post the words in the classroom
- During class literature discussions, ask students to describe how the character feels and why he or she feels that way. Asking students to make a face or pantomime to show how a character in a story feels will help students to learn about nonverbal communication.
- Monitor students' feelings by asking them to identify how they feel on a scale of 1–10. Ask a few students to share why they feel the way they do.
- Twice-exceptional students can learn a great deal from studying biographies of famous people with disabilities. Ask your students to compare characteristics and discuss how the famous person overcame his or her disability.
- Examine how famous people have experienced failure after failure before they finally succeeded. Have your students research mistakes that resulted in great inventions like Post-It Notes, Coca Cola, Scotch Guard, Silly Putty, penicillin, and the pacemaker.

SENSITIVITY, INTENSITY, AND EMOTIONALITY

From an early age, gifted learners are concerned with issues of fairness and morality (Grobman, 2006). Many are sensitive to the pain of others and can become intensely concerned with issues such as impoverished children in Africa, the morality of war, or an unjust way someone was treated by others. This sensitivity is a part of who they are and their concerns should not simply be dismissed. Assist students in finding ways to ease the pain of others or deal with issues of fairness and morality. They can head up a program to welcome new students to the school, work on an antibullying campain, collect toys for disadvantaged children, or gather food for a community pantry.

Gifted learners can become passionately interested in a particular topic and have an intense desire to study the topic in greater depth and complexity. Try to be flexible and use strategies like curriculum compacting to free up time for these students to study their passion areas. Search for appropriate audiences where students can share what they have learned. For example, Tim was passionately interested in dinosaurs. His intense interest became a problem when teachers wanted him to study other curriculum areas and peers were annoyed by his narrow interests. I overheard a peer tell him that he was too old to be interested in dinosaurs. After this, I invited a paleontologist to speak to my class. Tim amazed our guest speaker and his classmates with his knowledge. The speaker invited him to go to the museum to work with him on his current project. Tim continues

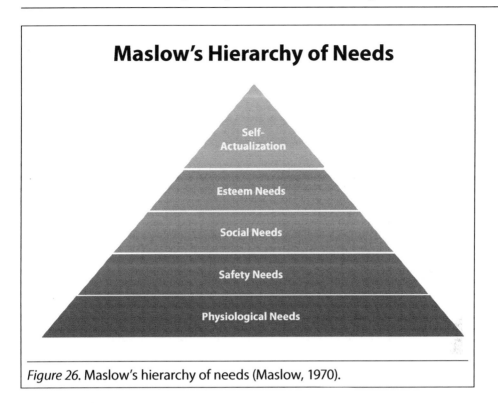

Figure 26. Maslow's hierarchy of needs (Maslow, 1970).

to work with his mentor at the museum, and his peers are no longer critical of his interest in dinosaurs.

Gifted students also can be extremely sensitive to the criticism of peers, parents, and teachers. For example, Paula received an A- on her report card in writing. For 2 weeks, she did not hand in a single writing assignment. She internalized her feelings, becoming anxious, withdrawn, and depressed. For weeks she perseverated, working for hours trying to write sentences for her spelling words, but she thought none of her sentences were good enough to hand in for a grade. On her way to school every morning she cried, explaining to her mother that the teacher hated her and she did not want to go to school. Thinking something terrible must have happened at school, her mother confronted the teacher. Needless to say, the teacher was a little annoyed by the mother's accusatory tone and Paula's overreaction to the A-. It was only Paula's perception that the teacher thought she was not a good writer. It was not until her teacher told her that she had given her an A- to leave room for growth that Paula was able to write with confidence again.

Hierarchy of Needs

Addressing the emotional needs of twice-exceptional learners is just as important or perhaps even more important than their academic needs. Programming for twice-exceptional learners must address a Hierachy of Needs as defined by Maslow (1954) and illustrated in Figure 26.

This Hierachy of Needs continues to be relevant today. These needs must be met for students to achieve self-actualization. The following is a detailed explanation of those needs:

- Physiological needs are our basic survival needs for food, water, and shelter. This is a problem for some students, and it is very difficult to concentrate on school work when you do not know where you are going to be sleeping that night.
- Safety needs represent the needs for security, law and order, freedom from fear, and the need for stability. Students who are bullied in school or live in fear that they will fail in school are at risk.
- Social needs are not achieved by students who feel different, do not have friends, or do not have a sense of connection with school. Students who have friends and affiliations with school are less likely to drop out.
- Esteem needs are our needs to achieve and be recognized for our contributions. They include our need to be viewed as unique individuals who are independent and capable.
- Self-actualization is the need for fulfillment, to have purpose and meaning in life. It is the need to be creative and realize inner potential. Twice-exceptional learners need a chance to develop their potential.

Emotional Distress

Discrepancies between their abilities, the presence of disabilities, and unrealistic expectations can result in repeated failure (King, 2005). This diminishes twice-exceptional learners' self-concepts (Waldron et al., 1987). It can lead these gifted students to have conflicted feelings about their abilities. Their anxiety increases as they try to meet their unrealistic expectations and perceived expectations of others. As a result, they suffer from extreme frustation, fear of failure, and a heightened sense of inefficacy (Baum, 1984a). When these students are under extreme stress, they can lose focus and become distracted, their ability to concentrate breaks down, and they develop eccentric behaviors (Grobman, 2009). Even though they are very bright, students in emotional crises are not able to deal with the demands of school. Their lack of achievement can send them into a downward spiral that can become critical in a short time span.

Evidence of their emotional distress can be displayed in disruptive or withdrawn behaviors (Baum et al., 1991), learned helplessness (Whitmore, 1980; Whitmore & Maker, 1985), and depression (Olenchak & Reis, 2002). Stress and negative experiences can result in behaviors that are internalized or externalized. Internalized behaviors appear as anxiety or depression while externalized behaviors are demonstrated by defiance, acting out, tantrums, or clowning behaviors. Externalized behaviors can become so significant that the student is identified with a behavioral or bipolar disorder. Internalized behaviors can manifest in depression and, in extreme instances, suicide. Unfortunately, the focus of interventions frequently becomes managing the behaviors and the underlying issues are never addressed. Interventions should focus on helping students learn how to deal with their frustration, emotionality, and sensitivity in socially acceptable ways.

Fight or Flight Responses

Repeated failures increase twice-exceptional students' frustration level and their emotionality can become very apparent. Negative experiences can result in a reptilian-like fight or flight response. While the reptilian-like brain controls their behavior, students are unable to think or problem solve. The ensuing out of control behaviors are alarming to teachers, parents, and peers. These behaviors diminish students' confidence in their ability to cope with the challenges of life.

Teachers must be really sensitive to situations that are stressful for twice-exceptional learners. Closely monitor students who are showing signs of extreme frustration or excessive stress. Have a prearranged strategy that you can implement quickly to get these students out of a stressful situation. Leaving the classroom, walking to the office, or having a casual conversation with the school secretary or nurse all will help to diminish students' stress levels and prevent the fight or flight responses from taking control. Later in the day, the teacher or a school counselor can meet with students to discuss the stressful event and reflect on what happened. Through discussion and reflection, students will gain an understanding of the issues that are causing the stress. This is a good time to talk about self-regulation and coping or calming strategies students can use.

Here are some tips for managing stressful or emotional situations:
1. Anticipate the Problem
   a. Be sensitive to situations that are stressful for the student.
   b. Look for clues of frustration that might trigger a meltdown.

2. Preplan an Intervention
   a. Plan a strategy that will remove the student from the situation that is causing the frustration.

3. Implement the Plan
   a. Quickly implement the plan when you notice the student is becoming frustrated and may be approaching a meltdown.

4. Reflect on the Event
   a. After the student has calmed down, reflect on what happened.
   b. Coach the student in developing self-regulation skills.

Self-Regulation Skills

Teach students to reflect on their own behavior and learn how to set personal goals and monitor their progress in meeting those goals. It is psychologically empowering when students realize they can take control of their learning and behaviors. Teach students to follow these steps to develop self-regulation skills:

1. Define the problem.
2. Explain your viewpoint.
3. Explain the other person's view point.
4. Brainstorm possible solutions.
5. Consider the consequences and select the best solution.

Functional Behavior Assessment (FBA)

A Functional Behavioral Assessment (FBA) will provide a comprehensive assessment of a student's behavior and why it occurs. For example, a student with dyslexia may act out in order to avoid reading out loud in class because she does not want other students to know she cannot read. A student with auditory processing deficits who has a difficult time understanding verbal information may prefer to be sent to the office rather than risk not being able to answer a question in class. A student with poor interpersonal skills may kick another student to get his attention because he does not know how to interact with peers.

A problem-solving team uses a systematic process to collect data from a variety of sources. These sources can include cognitive and academic assessments, observations, and interviews with teachers, parents, and students. The team considers the following to gain a comprehensive understanding of the problem:

1. *Antecedent events*: Observe and describe the events that occur before the problem behavior and trigger the behavior. Avoiding the antecedent event may stop the problem behavior.
2. *Problem behavior*: Observe the problem behavior and describe in detail the behavior, setting, frequency, and duration.
3. *Consequences*: Closely examine the positive consequences that occur as a result of the problem behavior. The student may be able to get a positive reaction from peers or a valued activity because of the behavior. Perhaps the behavior allows the student to avoid a difficult task or a classroom activity.

Positive Behavioral Intervention and Supports (PBIS)

PBIS is a process of collecting data and monitoring the behaviors of individuals and the behavior patterns within a school. The goal is to create a safe school environment that meets the individual needs of students. Individual students who need positive behavior instruction and support receive small-group interventions. Students whose behavior continues to be a problem participate in individualized intensive interventions. A behavior plan seeks to find ways of supporting desirable behavior rather than punishing undesirable behavior. It provides positive reinforcement to reward and support students in developing the appropriate or desirable behavior.

Emotional Problem Solving

Learning problem-solving strategies puts students in charge of their behavior, which increases their ability to overcome obstacles. Telling twice-exceptional learners that they could get good grades or could behave if only they would work harder only heightens anxiety levels and makes the situation worse. Teach students emotional problem-solving skills so they can learn how to take control of their behavior. I have adapted the emotional problem-solving process to be similar to the Creative Problem Solving process because it is beneficial for students to learn one process they can use to solve all of their problems.

The steps in emotional problem solving include:

1. Identify the problem.
2. Brainstorm possible solutions.
3. Select the best alternative.
4. Develop a plan.
5. Reflect on the outcome.

Teach this process to the entire class as a group learning experience. Have students identify a problem in the school they want to solve. Brainstorm possible solutions and learn the techniques of brainstorming as presented in Chapter 4. With the entire class, discuss how to select the best alternative. Develop and implement a plan and then reflect on the outcome. After the group training, coach students in using the problem-solving process to solve the problem they have selected.

Strategies for Relieving Emotional Distress
- Be alert to signs that students need a break and provide a safe place where the individual students can go when they are becoming frustrated or overwhelmed.
- Develop a plan ahead of time so you can respond quickly when students begin to lose control. For instance, ask individual students to deliver a note to the office. Prearrange this activity with the office so they will know what is going on. Students will get a break and will have a chance to calm down.

- Teach students self-regulation strategies, problem-solving routines, and emotional problem-solving strategies so they can take control their own behavior.

- Assist students in developing positive coping strategies such as seeking support, positive reappraisal, and accepting responsibility.

- Provide a safe place in the classroom or a discrete way for students to leave the classroom when they are stressed and need a break to cope.

SELF-CONCEPT AND SELF-ESTEEM

Self-concept is a complex, organized, dynamic system of learned beliefs, attitudes, and opinions a person holds related to his worth as an individual (Harter, Whitesell, & Junkin, 1998; Purkey, 1988). It continues to be shaped and reshaped throughout life by the successes and failures a person experiences. Frustrating school experiences, an anti-intellectual climate, and peer bullying negatively influence students' developing self-concept and self-esteem. The National Association for Self-Esteem defines self-esteem as feeling capable of meeting life's challenges and worthy of happiness (Reasoner, 2010). The way a person perceives himself will help predict his behavior and effectiveness (Betts, 1991). In other words, self-esteem is our inner voice telling us how we feel about ourselves. For some twice-exceptional learners, this inner voice becomes a harsh inner critic, criticizing and belittling their accomplishments. Students' views of their academic work strongly influence their self-concept and achievement (Winne, Woodlands, & Wong, 1982).

Through their life experiences, children learn to view themselves and their relationships with others. Experiences that are inconsistent with their self-concept are perceived as threats. The more inconsistent the experiences, the more rigid and resistive to change they become in an attempt to avoid activities that may result in failure and protect their fragile concept of self. These students can appear defiant or oppositional as they sit in class making minimal progress on assignments. Reactions toward students perceived as lazy are quite different than the more empathetic assistance hard-working students with a learning disability usually receive. Twice-exceptional learners can develop many creative and manipulative coping strategies as they try to avoid failure. Some students will become class clowns in an attempt to draw attention away from their weaknesses. Emotional problems arise when twice-exceptional learners cannot make sense of the perceived inconsistencies (Purkey, 1988). Social and emotional issues can have greater influences on students' achievement than their disabilities.

Students develop self-esteem when they are successful at something that they perceive as difficult (Rimm, 1986). As Greg told me, "A big problem for me with self-esteem was for a long time, I thought it was something you just got. It took me a long time to realize that self-esteem is usually something you had to earn for yourself." Positive feedback promotes the development of self-esteem and is one of the greatest sources of intrinsic motivation (Jensen, 1998). Acknowledging students' success positively influences their belief in themselves and their abilities. Teachers should provide the necessary scaffolding and support to ensure students will be successful and build on the students' successes to promote the development of positive self-esteem. When students engage in negative self-talk, ask them to stop, take three deep breaths, and visualize a specific time when they were successful.

Strategies to Increase Self-Esteem
- Provide a safe learning environment where diversity is respected and all students are valued for the contributions they can make.
- Encourage feelings of empathy within the classroom and never allow students to make negative remarks about other students.
- Differentiate instruction so content, process, and product matches the students' interests, abilities, and cognitive styles of processing information.
- Students should know that if they invest reasonable effort, they will be able to successfully complete assignments.
- Support and encourage students as they strive to achieve something that is difficult and celebrate their accomplishments when they succeed.

REALISTIC EXPECTATIONS AND GOAL SETTING

Learning to have realistic expectations is extremely difficult for twice-exceptional learners. They are advanced beyond their years in some areas and really struggle with other aspects of learning. On the one hand, they can come up with incredible solutions to problems, but are unable to implement the plan. Their internal inconsistencies can cause extreme frustration. They need challenging curriculum and differentiated instruction that provides adequate challenge to develop their gifted potential and support in their areas of weakness so they can be successful in school. If the challenge is too great, they will become frustrated and give up. When the curriculum does not provide enough challenge, they become bored and lose interest in learning. Teachers can help twice-exceptional students learn to have realistic expectations by providing the proper amount of challenge and support so they can successfully complete assignments and projects.

Strategies to Help Students Learn to Set Realistic Goals

- Teach students how to create and use an evaluation rubric to evaluate their own work. The students evaluate their work and then the teacher evaluates the work and they compare the results. Often the students' evaluations are more critical than the teacher's evaluation. The goal is for the students' and teacher's evaluations to be similar. It is particularly helpful for perfectionists to learn how to realistically evaluate their work.
- Coach students in setting realistic goals and help them learn how to break long-term goals into short-term goals. Celebrate effort, completion of homework, and attainment of goals. Provide opportunities for students to explore career and college options.

SUMMARY

Twice-exceptional learners exhibit characteristics of confusion, anxiety, hypersensitivity, frustration, perfectionism, and self-criticism. Their sensitivity, intensity, and emotionality make them vulnerable. Like other gifted students, they have high aspirations for success in their endeavors. However, hidden disabilities can make it difficult for twice-exceptional learners to achieve commensurate with their ability. They tend to set unrealistic goals and then get very upset when they cannot achieve them. These students are unable to meet their own expectations or the expectations of their parents or teachers. It is so important for twice-exceptional learners to gain an understanding and acceptance of their strengths, weaknesses, and learning styles. Learning to equate success with effort helps them to realize that they are in control of their future. They need coaching to learn to set realistic goals and support in their efforts to achieve those goals. The next chapter will examine how to develop a comprehensive plan with interventions designed to assist students in achieving their potential and becoming self-actualized.

Chapter 9

PUTTING THE PIECES TOGETHER

Twice-exceptional learners seem so capable when discussing issues they are passionate about, but they are often unorganized and sometimes defiant when it comes to completing homework. Many teachers believe these students could be successful in school if they were more responsible and tried a little harder. Most twice-exceptional learners want to be successful in school. It is not only skill deficits in academic subjects that prevents them from being successful in school, but personal characteristics like perfectionism and cognitive issues like executive functioning and processing speed that impair their abilities. Recent research has increased our understanding of twice-exceptional learners. In each of the chapters in this book, I have shared research on important components related to the education of twice-exceptional learners. Each component must be considered in the process of developing a comprehensive plan for twice-exceptional learners. Many plans fail because they just focus on one aspect of the problem, usually an area of weakness. When planning for twice-exceptional learners, the approach must be more comprehensive in scope, addressing the cognitive, academic, social, and emotional needs of the student. This chapter will guide educators through the process of creating a comprehensive plan for meeting the individual needs of twice-exceptional learners. Following these steps will improve academic, social, and emotional outcomes for twice-exceptional learners.

EXAMINING POSSIBILITIES

Twice-exceptional learners have amazing potential. So many famous scientists, mathematicians, musicians, and writers have overcome disabilities to become eminent in their fields of expertise. Dr. Carol Greider, a molecular biologist at Johns Hopkins University School of Medicine, recently was awarded the 2009 Nobel Prize for Medicine. She credits her early struggles with dyslexia for her success: "I think to a degree, it was my learning to overcome obstacles early in my life," said Greider (Mundy, 2009, p. 1). She discovered the enzyme telomerase that restores telomeres, the end caps on chromosomes, and protects them from damage. Telomerase and tolemeres are implicated in cancer and genetic diseases related to aging. Her visionary work continues to discover unforeseen connections. She credits dyslexia in part for her success. Dyslexia created obstacles over and above learning to read that Greider had to overcome. She learned persistence when realizing that the more she read, the easier it became. Placement in remedial classes resulted in self-esteem problems that were more difficult to overcome. When she applied to graduate schools, 8 of the 10 universities she applied to sent letters of rejection without even interviewing her. Even though she had wonderful letters of recommendation, great experiences, and excellent grades, standardized GRE scores were deemed to be a more important indicator of success (Mundy, 2009). Dr. Greider found a place where her abilities were valued and she had an opportunity to study, research, and develop her potential.

How many twice-exceptional learners with extraordinary abilities will simply drop out of school before their potential has had a chance to develop? I wonder what contributions these twice-exceptional learners with their unique perspectives and ability to think outside the box could have made.

IMPROVING OUTCOMES

In order to improve outcomes for twice-exceptional learners you must develop a comprehensive plan. The goal should be to maximize success and minimize failure. An effective plan provides the challenge students need to develop their gifted potential and the support they need to overcome their disabilities. The interventions provide instruction on the skills needed to be successful in school and the self-actualization skills necessary for developing potential. The plan should minimize risk factors and seek to support the development of resiliency, which acts as a protective buffer to shield students from adversity. It increases students' abilities to cope and overcome adversity. These factors contribute to positive self-esteem and self-efficacy and increase students' confidence in their ability to be successful. Students should play a major role in planning and developing intervention goals. Learning how to set smart goals is an important step toward self-actualization. In addition, twice-exceptional students need support and encouragement as they strive to achieve their goals. As students integrate their academic goals with their life goals, their intrinsic motivation increases. Teachers can play an important role in self-actualization by coaching students as they learn (a) to set realistic short- and long-term goals, (b) to plan the steps necessary to attain the goal, (c) to appraise the steps and results, and (e) to celebrate their successes.

Follow the steps below to develop a comprehensive plan that nurtures twice-exceptional students' gifted potential, supports their cognitive style, encourages academic achievement, fosters interpersonal relationships, and promotes intrapersonal understanding.

Step 1: Assemble a Collaborative Team

The classroom teacher needs support from gifted education and special education professionals when developing and implementing a plan for twice-exceptional learners. The home-school partnership and the students' involvement are crucial elements for success. Occupational therapists, reading/writing specialists, social workers, counselors, psychologists, and administrators may be asked to participate on the team based on the students' cognitive, academic, social, and emotional needs. Chapter 2 discussed the importance of bringing together a collaborative team so their combined expertise can guide the development, implementation, and monitoring of the comprehensive plan. That chapter also discussed the importance of the home-school partnership in this process.

Step 2: Collect and Analyze Data

A variety of qualitative and quantitative data that can be used to identify specific problems were discussed in greater depth in Chapter 3. Collect all available data and determine what additional data are required to get a comprehensive picture of the students' strengths and challenges. The following represent frequently used data:

- Universal screening, curriculum-based assessments or measurements, norm-referenced assessments, achievement tests, diagnostic assessments, Functional Behavioral Assessments, and diagnostic assessments can be used to collect assessment data.

- Observations, interviews, and portfolios provide valuable information and should be a part of data collection. Interviewing the students, their parents, and their teachers can be very effective to gain a better understanding of their perspectives.
- Checklists and scales like the Risk and Resiliency Continuum (Figure 7) and the Strengths and Challenges (Figure 8) checklist found in Chapter 3 provide valuable information needed in the development of a comprehensive plan. The Vineland Adaptive Behavior Scale, the Behavior Assessment System for Children (BASC), and the Gifted Rating Scales (GRS) are quick assessments frequently used for specific information.
- Cognitive assessments, as discussed in Chapter 5, provide information on cognitive processing, executive functioning, attention, and processing speed.

Step 3: Comprehensive Planning

Use the Twice-Exceptional Planning Continuums in the appendix as a guide when defining your students' needs and developing a comprehensive plan.

Nurture gifted potential.

Emphasis on developing strengths is a key element in meeting the educational needs of twice-exceptional students (Barton & Starnes, 1989; Baum et al., 1989; Baum & Owen, 1988; Whitmore & Maker, 1985). Twice-exceptional learners needed opportunities to use their advanced knowledge, abstract thinking, creativity, and reasoning skills in discussions, challenging projects, and real-world assignments (Baum et al., 2001). Challenging learning opportunities in their strength areas help to prevent the stress that results when there is inadequate academic challenge. Strength-based challenges motivate students to continue to want to learn. Teachers can play an essential role in mentoring the development of gifted potential by providing consistent challenge and opportunities to reflect on their progress (Rogers, 2007). Chapter 4 provided an in-depth discussion and strategies for nurturing potential that focus on differentiated instruction, emphasis on higher order thinking, and problem solving.

The Twice-Exceptional Planning Continuum for Nurturing Gifted Potential that can be found in the appendix will guide you through the planning process by asking you to:

1. Review the guiding principles before beginning.
2. Tally the results of the Strengths and Challenges checklist (Figure 8) completed previously. Fill in the number of times teachers and parents checked 1–5 for each statement. Determine if it is an area of strength or challenge for the student and place a S or C to the left of the statement.

3. Define what the student needs to develop his or her gifted potential and develop a SMART goal (see Step 8 below for more information).

4. Use the Intervention Continuum to Nurture Gifted Potential that can be found in the appendix to guide you in selecting appropriate interventions. These are just suggestions, so do not limit yourself to only these interventions. Select interventions that will help the students achieve their goals.

5. Answer the implementation questions.

The suggestions above apply for each of the following steps as well.

Support cognitive style.

Twice-exceptional learners have advanced cognitive abilities but can have deficits in skills that keep them from achieving their potential. Many twice-exceptional learners have significant cognitive discrepancies (Schiff et al., 1981). They may have auditory, visual, or processing speed deficits that can interfere with their ability to process information and can negatively influence achievement. Executive functioning skills are necessary for students to be able to plan, prioritize, and organize homework assignments, but the development of these skills develops more slowly. Preferred learning styles can influence the way students think, process information, and learn. Nonlinear thinking styles and high levels of creativity make it difficult for these students to learn when taught in a sequential step-by-step process. Their learning can be hindered by problems with short-term memory, attention, hyperactivity, and sensory integration. Chapter 5 provided an in-depth discussion of cognitive processing and suggestions for interventions.

The Twice-Exceptional Planning Continuum for Supporting Cognitive Style that can be found in the appendix will guide you through the planning process for this step.

Encourage academic achievement.

Hidden disabilities and inappropriate educational conditions contribute to underachievement in twice-exceptional learners (Reis & McCoach, 2002). Research has shown it is not good practice to focus on weaknesses because it results in poor self-esteem, lack of motivation, depression, and stress (Baum, 1984b; Whitmore & Maker, 1985). Twice-exceptional learners achieve when teachers emphasized developing their strengths, while at the same time, provided explicit instruction relative to their weaknesses (Barton & Starnes, 1989; Baum et al., 1998; Baum & Owen, 1988; Whitmore & Maker, 1985). It is important to identify the skill deficits that are negatively impacting students' school performance and provide explicit instruction so they can develop the skills they need to be successful. Providing the support and encouragement twice-exceptional students need is essential for them to learn how to persist through their struggles. Chapter 6 examined risk and resiliency factors that influence achievement and provided strategies educators can use to assist students who struggle with dyslexia, dysgraphia, and dyscalculia.

The Twice-Exceptional Planning Continuum for Encouraging Academic Achievement that can be found in the appendix will guide you through the planning process for this step.

Foster interpersonal relationships.

Difficulties with social skills, generating solutions to social problems, and interpreting social cues (Stormont et al., 2001) lead to feeling different and isolated (King, 2005; Nielsen & Higgins, 2005). Twice-exceptional learners often equate feelings of being different with being "strange" or "unacceptable." Because they are unusually sensitive, they take the teasing and criticism of others to heart and this becomes the basis of their self-concept (Silverman, 2003). Normal social development depends on the ability to identify and bond with others. Failure to develop positive peer relationships means twice-exceptional learners are unable to complete a basic developmental task. It can lead to social and emotional consequences that can profoundly affect their future (Goerss, 2005). Conflicts with teachers occur when teachers do not understand why students are unable to complete assignments. Misinterpreting their apparent lack of motivation as defiance or laziness, teachers can take a punitive approach when what these students need is a more empathetic approach. Parents can further complicate the issue when they try to intervene and become enablers rather than empowering their children to overcome their disabilities. Chapter 7 provided a more in-depth discussion of these issues and strategies to assist students in developing interpersonal skills.

The Twice-Exceptional Planning Continuum for Fostering Interpersonal Relationships that can be found in the appendix will guide you through the planning process for this step.

Promote intrapersonal understanding.

Dealing with both exceptionalities is confusing (King, 2005) and frustrating (Coleman, 2001). Dysfunctional perfectionism, intensity of emotions (Silverman, 1989), oversensitivity, low self-esteem, intense frustration with difficult tasks, disruptive or withdrawn behaviors (Baum et al., 1991), and depression (Olenchak & Reis, 2002) are issues that twice-exceptional learners must learn to overcome. Academic and personal success depends more on normal social and emotional development than on curriculum (Goerss, 2005). Twice-exceptional learners need opportunities to develop a greater awareness, understanding, and acceptance of self that is essential for positive growth (Betts, 1991). Effective personal habits, good attitudes, social competence, and emotional stability all depend on social and emotional learning and maturation. If normal social and emotional tasks are not accomplished, the best curriculum in the world will not make up for the resulting struggles (Goerss, 2005). Chapter 8 provided strategies to empower twice-exceptional students by helping them to reach the awareness, understanding, and acceptance they need to successfully develop their potential and learn to persist in reaching realistic goals.

The Twice-Exceptional Planning Continuum for Promoting Intrapersonal Understanding that can be found in the appendix will guide you through the planning process.

Step 4: Develop SMART Goals

SMART goals are written to describe the desired results, how the results will be measured, and when the goal will be attained. I recommend teaching students how to develop smart goals and guide them in developing the goals for their IEP. After all it is their life and learning to set goals and working to achieve them is a valuable lesson. In order for goals to be smart, they must be:

- *Specific*: Make sure the goals define what needs to be done. They need to be detailed, concise, and clear.
- *Measurable*: Goals should contain a numeric or descriptive measure you can use to determine if you have attained your goal. Instead of students saying, "I want to improve my grades," have students target a particular grade point average.
- *Achievable*: It is important for students to learn how to set goals that are realistic and achievable. Make sure the students have the resources and support they need to achieve their goal.
- *Relevant*: Goals need to focus on a clear outcome, product, or accomplishment.
- *Time-Bound*: Identify a target specific date when the goal will be achieved.

Step 5: Putting It All Together

Summarize the information from the Twice-Exceptional Planning Continuums on the 2-page form titled Twice-Exceptional Education Plan (found in the appendix).

Step 6: Implement, Monitor, and Modify

Implement the plan and monitor the students' progress at regular intervals to make sure they are making adequate progress. Modify the plan according to the students' needs and progress by increasing or decreasing the level of interventions.

The students' progress has to be monitored at regular intervals to make sure they are making adequate progress. The plan is modified according to progress the students are making by increasing or decreasing the level of intervention.

CONCLUSION

Twice-exceptional learners continue to be at risk in an education system that does not understand their diverse needs. In reality, interventions are rarely provided for either their gifted potential or their disabilities in the primary grades because they are able to compensate for their disability and achieve grade-level standards. As twice-exceptional learners progress through school, they experience extreme frustration trying to deal with both of their exceptionalities. Delays in the recognition of their exceptionality can result in social and emotional consequences that can be very debilitating. The incidence of underachievement and the dropout rate for this special population is undocumented but considered to be significant. The implementation of Response to Intervention (RtI) provides an opportunity to address the needs of twice-exceptional learners when they first begin to struggle in school. Early interventions will reduce the frustration twice-exceptional learners experience in school and the social and emotional issues that occur when interventions are delayed.

This book was written to guide educators in developing a comprehensive plan for meeting the diverse needs of twice-exceptional learners using the RtI framework and the problem-solving process. I purposefully included planning guides to guide collaborative teams step-by-step through the process of developing a plan in order to help administrators and educators serve those twice-exceptional learners in their schools appropriately. I also included forms to guide teams in designing a plan to nurture gifted potential, support cognitive style, encourage academic achievement, foster interpersonal relationships, and promote intrapersonal understanding. Specific intervention strategies were detailed in each chapter along with suggestions for a continuum of intervention so the plan can be tailored to individual needs. My hope is that educators will use these materials and improve outcomes for twice-exceptional learners. Best of luck to you as you serve the twice-exceptional students in your school or classroom.

REFERENCES

Adderholdt-Elliott, M. (1987). *Perfectionism: What's bad about being too good?* Minneapolis, MN: Free Spirit.

Adelman, H. S. (1992). The next 25 years. *Journal of Learning Disabilities, 25*, 17–22.

Aiex, N. K. (1993). *Bibliotherapy* (Report No. EDO-CS-93-05). Bloomington, IN: ERIC Clearinghouse on Reading, English, and Communication.

American Psychiatric Association. (2000). *Diagnostic and statistical manual of mental disorders* (4th ed., Text rev.). Washington, DC: Author.

Ayres, A. J. (1972). *Sensory integration and learning disorders.* Los Angeles, CA: Western Psychological Services.

Barton, J. M., & Starnes, W. T. (1989). Identifying distinguishing characteristics of gifted and talented/learning disabled students. *Roeper Review, 12*, 23–29.

Baum, S. M. (1984a). Meeting the needs of learning disabled gifted students. *Roeper Review, 7*, 16–19.

Baum, S. M. (1984b). Recognizing special talents in learning disabled students. *Teaching Exceptional Children, 16*(2), 92–98.

Baum, S. M. (1990). *Gifted but learning disabled: A puzzling paradox* (ERIC Digest No. E479). Reston, VA: Council for Exceptional Children.

Baum, S. M. (1997). *Project high hopes: Final evaluation report* (No. R206R00001). Washington, DC: Office of Educational Research and Improvement.

Baum, S. M., Cooper, C. R., & Neu, T. W. (2001). Dual differentiation: An approach for meeting the curricular needs of gifted students with learning disabilities. *Psychology in the Schools, 38*, 477–490.

Baum, S. M., Emerick, L. J., Herman, G. N., & Dixon, J. (1989). Identification, programs and enrichment strategies for gifted learning disabled youth. *Roeper Review, 12*, 48–53.

Baum, S. M., Olenchak, F. R., & Owen, S. V. (1998). Gifted students with attention deficits: Fact and/or fiction? Or, can we see the forest for the trees? *Gifted Child Quarterly, 42*, 96–104.

Baum, S. M., & Owen, S. V. (1988). High ability/learning disabled students: How are they different? *Gifted Child Quarterly, 32*, 311–316.

Baum, S. M., Owen, S. V., & Dixon, J. (1991). *To be gifted and learning disabled: From identification to practical intervention strategies.* Mansfield Center, CT: Creative Learning Press.

Baum, S. M., Renzulli, J. S., & Hébert, T. (1995). *The prism metaphor: A new paradigm for reversing underachievement.* Storrs: The University of Connecticut, The National Research Center on the Gifted and Talented.

Beckley, D. (1998). *Gifted and learning disabled: Twice exceptional students.* Retrieved from http://www.sp.uconn.edu/~nrcgt/news/spring98/sprng984.html

Bender, W. N., Rosenkrans, C. B., & Crane, M. (1999). Stress, depression, and suicide among students with learning disabilities: Assessing the risk. *Learning Disabilities Quarterly, 22*, 143–156.

Betts, G. T. (1985). *The autonomous learner model for the gifted and talented.* Greeley, CO: ALPS.

Betts, G. T. (1991). The autonomous learner model for gifted and talented. In N. Colangelo & G. A. Davis (Eds.), *Handbook of gifted education* (3rd ed., pp. 142–153). Boston, MA: Allyn & Bacon.

Betts, G. T., & Kercher, J. K. (1999). *The autonomous learner model: Optimizing ability.* Greeley, CO: ALPS.

Bianco, M. (2005). The effects of disability labels on special education and general education teachers' referrals for gifted programs. *Learning Disability Quarterly, 28*, 285–293.

Board of Education of the Hendrick Hudson Central School District v. Rowley (80-1002), 458 U.S. 176 (1982).

Boodoo, G. M., Bradley, C. L., Frontera, R. L., Pitts, J. R., & Wright, L. B.

(1989). A survey of procedures used for identifying gifted learning disabled children. *Gifted Child Quarterly, 33,* 110–114.

Brody, L. E., & Mills, C. J. (1997). Gifted children with learning disabilities: A review of the issues. *Journal of Learning Disabilities, 30,* 282–286.

Brown v. Board of Education of Topeka, 347 U.S. 483 (1954).

Burks, B. S., Jensen, D. W., & Terman, L. M. (1930). *Genetic studies of genius, Vol. 3: The promise of youth: Follow-up studies of a thousand gifted children.* Stanford, CA: Stanford University Press.

Bush, G. (2008). Neuroimaging of Attention Deficit Hyperactivity Disorder: Can new imaging findings be integrated in clinical practice? *Child and Adolescent Psychiatric Clinics of North America, 17,* 385–404.

Cauce, A. M., Felner, R. D., & Primavera, J. (1982). Social support in high-risk adolescents: Structural components and adaptive impact. *American Journal of Community Psychology, 10,* 417–428.

Coffield, F., Moseley, D., Hall, E., & Ecclestone, K. (2004). *Learning styles and pedagogy in post-16 learning: A systematic and critical review.* London, England: Learning and Skills Research Center.

Cline, S., & Hedgeman, K. (2001). Gifted children with disabilities. *Gifted Child Today, 24*(3), 16–24.

Cline, S., & Schwartz, D. (1999). *Diverse populations of gifted children.* Upper Saddle River, NJ: Merrill/Prentice Hall.

Cohen, S., & Wills, T. A. (1985). Stress, social support, and the buffering hypothesis. *Psychological Bulletin, 98,* 310–357.

Colangelo, N. (2003). Counseling gifted students. In N. Colangelo & G. A. Davis (Eds.), *Handbook of gifted education* (pp. 3–9). Boston, MA: Allyn & Bacon.

Coleman, M. R. (1992). A comparison of how gifted/LD and average/LD boys cope with school frustration. *Journal for the Education of the Gifted, 15,* 239–265.

Coleman, M. R. (2001). Surviving or thriving? *Gifted Child Today, 24*(3), 56–64.

Coleman, M. R. (2005). Academic strategies that work for gifted students with learning disabilities. *Teaching Exceptional Children, 38*(1), 28–32.

Coleman, M. R., Harradine, C., & King, E. W. (2005). Meeting the needs of students who are twice-exceptional. *Teaching Exceptional Children, 38*(1), 5–6.

Conners, C. K. (1997). *Conners Rating Scales–Revised.* San Antonio, TX: Pearson Education.

Davis, G. A. (1998). *Creativity is forever.* Dubuque, IA: Kendall Hunt.

Davis, G. A., & Rimm, S. B. (2004). *Education of the gifted and talented* (5th ed.). Needham Heights, MA: Allyn & Bacon.

Deno, S. (2009). *Ongoing student assessment.* Retrieved from http://www.rtinetwork.org/essential/assessment/ongoingassessment

DiMatties, M. E., & Sammons, J. H. (2003). *Understanding sensory integra-*

tion. Reston, VA: Eric Clearinghouse on Disabilities and Gifted Education. (ERIC Document Reproduction Service No. ED478564)

Dole, S. (2000). The implications of the risk and resiliency literature for gifted students with learning disabilities. *Roeper Review, 23*, 91–96.

Durden, W. G., & Tangherlini, A. E. (1993). *Smart kids: How academic talents are developed and nurtured in America*. Kirkland, WA: Hogrefe & Huber.

Dweck, C. S. (1986). Motivation processes affecting learning. *American Psychologist, 41*, 1040–1048.

Dyslexia—Einstein. (n.d.) Retrieved from http://lucarinfo.com/inspire/deinstein.html

Education for All Handicapped Children Act of 1975, Pub. Law 94-142 (November 29, 1975).

Elementary and Secondary Education Act of 1965, §142, 20 U.S.C. 863.

Fall, J., & Nolan, L. (1993). A paradox of exceptionalities. *Gifted Child Today, 16*(1), 46–49.

Feldman, D. H. (1992). Has there been a paradigm shift in gifted education?: Some thoughts on a changing national scene. In N. Colangelo, S. G. Assouline, & D. L. Ambroson (Eds.), *Talent development: Proceedings from 1991 Henry and Jocelyn Wallace National Research Symposium on Talent Development* (pp. 89–94). Unionville, NY: Trillium.

Folkman, S., & Lazarus, R. (1988). *Ways of coping questionnaire*. Palo Alto, CA: Counseling Psychologist Press.

Fox, L. H., Brody, L., & Tobin, D. (1983). *Learning disabled/gifted children: Identification and programming*. Baltimore, MD: University Park Press.

Fuchs, D., & Fuchs, L. S. (2005). Responsiveness-to-intervention: A blueprint for practitioners, policymakers, and parents. *Teaching Exceptional Children, 38*, 57–61.

Fuchs, D., Mock, D., Morgan, P. L., & Young, C. L. (2003). Responsiveness-to-intervention: Definitions, evidence, and implications for the learning disabilities construct. *Learning Disabilities Research and Practice, 18*, 157–171.

Gagne, F. (2000). Understanding the complex choreography of talent development. In K. A. Heller, F. J. Mönks, R. J. Sternberg, & R. F. Subotnik (Eds.), *International handbook of giftedness and talent* (pp. 67–79). Amsterdam, The Netherlands: Elsevier.

Gallagher, J., & Harradine, C. C. (1997). Gifted students in the classroom. *Roeper Review, 19*, 132–136.

Gardner, H. (1999). *Intelligence reframed: Multiple intelligences for the 21st century*. New York, NY: Basic Books.

Garmezy, N. (1991). Resiliency and vulnerability to adverse developmental outcomes associated with poverty. *American Behavioral Scientist, 34*, 416–430.

Gazzaniga, M. (1988). *Mind matters: How mind and brain interact to create our conscious lives*. Boston, MA: Houghton-Mifflin/MIT Press.

Gerber, P. J., Ginsberg, R., & Reiff, H. B. (1992). Identifying alterable patterns in employment success for highly successful adults with learning disabilities. *Journal of Learning Disabilities, 25*, 475–487.

Goerss, J. (2005). *Director's corner: Asynchronous development.* Retrieved from http://www.sengifted.org/articles_directorscorner/Goerss_Aug05.shtml

Goldberg, E. (2001). *The executive brain: Frontal lobes and the civilized mind.* New York, NY: Oxford University Press.

Graner, P. S., Faggella-Luby, M. N., & Fritschmann, N. S. (2005). An overview of responsiveness to intervention: What practitioners ought to know. *Topics in Language Disorders, 25*, 93–105.

Grimm, J. (1998). The participation of gifted students with disabilities in gifted programs. *Roeper Review, 20*, 285–286.

Grobman, J. (2006). Underachievement in exceptionally gifted adolescents and young adults: A psychiatrist's view. *Journal of Secondary Gifted Education, 17*, 199–210.

Grobman, J. (2009). A psychodynamic psychotherapy approach to the emotional problems of exceptionally and profoundly gifted adolescents and adults: A psychiatrist's experience. *Journal for the Education of Gifted, 33*, 106–125.

Gross, M. U. M. (1998). The "me" behind the mask: Intellectually gifted students and the search for identity. *Roeper Review, 20*(3), 1–14.

Hannah, C. L., & Shore, B. M. (1995). Metacognition and high intellectual ability: Insight from the study of learning disabled gifted students. *Gifted Child Quarterly, 39*, 95–110.

Harter, S., Whitesell, N. R., & Junkin, L. J. (1998). Similarities and differences in domain-specific and global self-evaluations of learning-disabled, behaviorally disordered, and normally achieving adolescents. *American Educational Research Journal, 35*, 653–680.

Hartnett, D. N., Nelson, J. M., & Rinn, A. N. (2004). Gifted or ADD/ADHD? The possibilities of misdiagnosis. *Roeper Review, 26*, 73–76.

Henderson, A., Johnson, V., Mapp, K., & Davies, D. (2006). *Beyond the bake sale: The essential guide to family/school partnerships.* New York, NY: The New Press.

Higgins, L. D., & Nielsen, M. E. (1999, April). *Meeting the needs of twice-exceptional students: Programs that work.* Paper presented at the Council for Exceptional Children Annual Conference, Charlotte, NC.

Hishinuma, E., & Tadaki, S. (1996). Addressing diversity of the gifted/at risk: Characteristics for identification. *Gifted Child Today, 19*(5), 20–25, 28–29, 45, 50.

Hoffman, J. L., Wasson, F. R., & Christianson, B. P. (1985). Personal development for the gifted underachiever. *Gifted Child Today, 8*(3), 12–14.

Individuals with Disabilities Education Act, 20 U.S.C. §1401 et seq. (1990).

Individuals with Disabilities Education Improvement Act, Pub. Law 108-446 (December 3, 2004).

Jacobs, W. J., & Nadel, L. (1985). Stress-induced recovery of fears and phobias. *Psychological Review, 92,* 512–531.

Jensen, E. (1998). *Teaching with the brain in mind.* Alexandria, VA: Association for Supervision and Curriculum Development.

Johnson, L. J., Karnes, M. B., & Carr, V. W. (Eds.). (1997). *Providing services to children with gifts and disabilities: A critical need* (2nd ed.). Needham Heights, MA: Allyn & Bacon.

Karnes, F. A., Shaunessy, E., & Bislan, A. (2004). Gifted students with disabilities: Are we finding them? *Gifted Child Today, 27*(4), 16–21.

Kaufman, A. S. (1979). *Intelligent testing with the WISC-R.* New York, NY: Wiley.

Kauffman, J. M. (1993). *Characteristics of emotional and behavioral disorders of children and youth* (5th ed.). New York, NY: Macmillan Publishing.

Kibby, M. Y., Marks, W., Morgan, S., & Long, C. J. (2004). Specific impairment in developmental reading disabilities: A working memory approach. *Journal of Learning Disabilities, 37,* 349–363.

King, E. W. (2005). Addressing the social and emotional needs of twice exceptional students. *Teaching Exceptional Children, 38*(1), 16–20.

Knoblauch, B., & Sorenson, B. (1998). *IDEA's definition of disabilities* (ERIC Digest No. E560). Reston, VA: ERIC Clearinghouse on Disabilities and Gifted Education.

Kranowitz, C. S. (1998). *The out-of-sync child: Recognizing and coping with sensory integration dysfunction.* New York, NY: The Berkley Publishing Group.

La Morte, M. W. (2005). *School law: Cases and concepts* (8th ed.). New York, NY: Pearson.

Luthar, S. S., & Zigler, E. (1991). Vulnerability and competence: A review of research on resiliency in childhood. *American Orthopsychiatric, 61,* 6–22.

Lyytinen, H., Aro, M., Eklund, K., Erskine, J., Guttorm, T., Laakso, M., . . . Torppa, M. (2004). The development of children at familial risk for dyslexia: Birth to early school age. *Annals of Dyslexia, 54,* 184–220.

Maker, C. J. (1977). *Providing programs for the gifted handicapped.* Reston, VA: Council for Exceptional Children.

Maker, C. J. (1982). *Curriculum development for the gifted.* Rockville, MD: Aspen.

Maker, C. J., & Udall, A. J. (1985). *Giftedness and learning disabilities.* Retrieved from http://www.casenex.com/casenex/ericReadings/GiftednessAndLearning.pdf

Mann, V. A., & Foy, J. C. (2003). Phonological awareness, speech development, and letter knowledge in preschool children. *Annals of Dyslexia, 53,* 149–173.

Marland, S. P. (1972). *Education of the gifted and talented: Report to the Congress of the United States by the U.S. Commissioner of Education.* Washington, DC: U.S. Government Printing Office.

Maslow, A. H. (1954). *Motivation and personality.* New York, NY: Harper and Row.

Maslow, A. H. (1970). *Motivation and personality* (2nd ed.). New York, NY: Harper and Row.

McCarthy, B. (1980). *The 4 mat system.* Arlington Heights, IL: Excel.

McGreevey, A. (1992). All in the golden afternoon: The early life of Charles L. Dodgson (Lewis Carroll). *Gifted Child Quarterly, 36,* 6–10.

Mills v. Board of Education, DC, 348 F. Supp. 866 (D. DC 1972).

Miner, M., & Siegel, L. S. (1992). William Butler Yeats: Dyslexic? *Journal of Learning Disabilities, 25,* 372–375.

Moon, S., M. (2006). Developing a definition of giftedness. In J. H. Purcell & R. D. Eckert (Eds.), *Designing services and programs for high-ability learners: A guidebook for gifted education* (pp. 23–31). Thousand Oaks, CA: Corwin Press.

Mundy, L. (2009). *Success is in her DNA.* Retrieved from http://www.washingtonpost.com/wp-dyn/content/article/2009/10/19/AR2009101903328.html

Muscott, H. S., Szczesiul, S., Berk, B., Staub, K., Hoover, J., & Perry-Chisholm, P. (2008). Creating home-school partnerships by engaging families in school-wide positive behavior supports. *Teaching Exceptional Children, 40*(6), 6–14.

National Association for Gifted Children. (n.d.a). *NAGC position papers.* Retrieved from http://www.nagc.org/index2.aspx?id=375

National Association for Gifted Children. (n.d.b). *The history of gifted and talented education.* Retrieved from http://www.nagc.org/index.aspx?id=607

National Association for Gifted Children. (n.d.c). *What is giftedness?* Retrieved from http://www.nagc.org/index.aspx?id=574&ir

National Center on Response to Intervention. (2009). *Progress monitoring tools chart: Reading and math.* Retrieved from http://www.rti4success.org/chart/progressMonitoring/PMToolsChart_04-20-10a.pdf

National Center on Response to Intervention. (2010). *Screening tools chart.* Retrieved from http://www.rti4success.org/chart/screeningTools/ScreeningToolsChart_052010.pdf

National Institute of Child Health and Human Development. (2000). *Report of the National Reading Panel. Teaching children to read: An evidence-based assessment of the scientific research literature on reading and its implications for reading instruction* (NIH Publication No. 00-4769). Washington, DC: U.S. Government Printing Office.

Neihart, M. (1999). The impact of giftedness on psychological well-being: What does the empirical literature say? *Roeper Review, 22,* 278–319.

Nettle, S. M., Mucherah, W., & Jones, D. S. (2000). Understanding resilience: The role of social resources. *Journal of Education for Students Placed At Risk, 5*(1 & 2), 47–60.

Nicholson, C. L., & Alcorn, C. L. (1994). *Educational applications of the WISC-III: A handbook of interpretive strategies and remedial recommendations.* Los Angeles, CA: Western Psychological Services.

Nielsen, M. E. (1989). *The twice-exceptional child project* (Javits Grant No. R206A90151). Washington, DC: U.S. Department of Education.

Nielsen, M. E. (1993). *Project reach: Addressing the needs of twice-exceptional learners* (Javits Grant No. R206A30259). Washington, DC: U. S. Department of Education.

Nielsen, M. E. (2002). Gifted students with learning disabilities: Recommendations for identification and programming. *Exceptionality, 10*(2), 93–111.

Nielsen, M. E., & Higgins, L. D. (2005). The eye of the storm services and programs for twice-exceptional learners. *Teaching Exceptional Children, 38*(1), 8–15.

Oden, M. (1968). The fulfillment of promise: 40-year follow-up of the Terman gifted group. *Genetic Psychology Monographs, 77*, 3–93.

Olenchak, F. R. (1994). Talent development: Accommodating the social and emotional needs of secondary gifted learning disabled students. *Journal of Secondary Gifted Education, 5*, 40–52.

Olenchak, F. R., & Reis, S. M. (2002). Gifted students with learning disabilities. In M. Neihart, S. M. Reis, N. M. Robinson, & S. M. Moon (Eds.), *The social and emotional development of gifted children: What do we know?* (pp. 177–189). Waco, TX: Prufrock Press.

Papanicolaou, A. C., Simos, P. G., Breier, J. I., Fletcher, J. M., Foorman, B. R., Francis, D., . . . Davis, R. N. (2003). Brain mechanisms for reading in children with and without dyslexia: A review of studies of normal development and plasiticity. *Developmental Neuropsychology, 24*(3), 593–612.

Pashler, H., McDaniel, M., Rohrer, D., & Bjork, R. (2009). Learning styles. *Psychological Science in the Public Interest, 9*, 105–119.

Pennsylvania Association for Retarded Citizens v. Commonwealth of Pennsylvania, 334 F. Supp. 1257 (E.D. Pa. 1971).

Pianta, R., & Walsh, D. J. (1998). Applying the construct of resilience in schools: Cautions from a developmental system perspective. *School Psychology Review, 27*, 407–417.

Pikulski, J. J., & Chard, D. J. (2005). Fluency: Bridge between decoding and reading comprehension. *The Reading Teacher, 58*, 510–519.

Purkey, W. W. (1988). *An overview of self-concept theory for counselors.* Ann Arbor, MI: ERIC Clearinghouse on Counseling and Personnel Services. (ERIC Document Reproduction Service No. ED304630)

Reasoner, R. (2010). *The true meaning of self-esteem.* Retrieved from http://www.self-esteem-nase.org/what.php

Reid, B. D., & McGuire, M. D. (1995). *Square pegs in round holes—These kids don't fit: High ability students with behavioral problems* (RBDM 9512). Storrs: The University of Connecticut, The National Research Center on the Gifted and Talented.

Reis, S. M., & McCoach, B. D. (2002). Underachievement in gifted and talented students with special needs. *Exceptionality, 10,* 113–125.

Reis, S. M., & Neu, T. W. (1994). Factors involved in the academic success of high ability university students with learning disabilities. *Journal of Secondary Gifted Education, 5,* 60–74.

Reis, S. M., Neu, T. W., & McGuire, J. (1995). *Talent in two places: Case studies of high ability students with learning disabilities who have achieved* (Research Monograph 95114). Storrs: The University of Connecticut, The National Research Center on the Gifted and Talented.

Renzulli, J. S. (1978). What makes giftedness? Reexamining a definition. *Phi Delta Kappan, 60,* 180–184.

Renzulli, J. S., & Reis, S. M. (1985). *The schoolwide enrichment model: A comprehensive plan for educational excellence.* Mansfield Center, CT: Creative Learning Press.

Reynolds, M. C., Zetlin, A. G., & Wang, M. C. (1993). 20/20 Analysis: Taking a close look at the margins. *Exceptional Children, 59,* 294–300.

Riding, R. J. (1997). On the nature of cognitive style. *Educational Psychology, 17,* 29–50.

Ridley, D. S., Schutz, P. A., Glanz, R. S., & Weinstein, C. E. (1992). Self-regulated learning: The interactive influence of metacognitive awareness and goal-setting. *Journal of Experimental Education, 60,* 293–306.

Rimm, S. (1986). *Underachievement syndrome: Causes and cures.* Watertown, WI: Apple.

Rimm, S. (1989). *Why bright kids get poor grades: And what you can do about it.* New York, NY: Three Rivers Press.

Rogers, K. B. (2002). *Re-forming gifted education: How parents and teachers can match the program to the child.* Scottsdale, AZ: Great Potential Press.

Rogers, K. B. (2007). Lessons learned about educating the gifted and talented: A synthesis of the research on educational practice. *Gifted Child Quarterly, 51,* 382–396.

Schiff, M. M., Kaufman, A. S., & Kaufman, N. L. (1981). Scatter analysis of WISC-R profiles for learning disabled children with superior intelligence. *Journal of Learning Disabilities, 14,* 400–404.

Schunk, D. H. (1984). Sequential attributional feedback and children's achievement behaviors. *Journal of Educational Psychology, 75,* 511–518.

Scruggs, T. E., & Mastropieri, M. A. (2002). On babies and bathwater: Addressing the problems of identification of learning disabilities. *Learning Disabilities Quarterly, 25,* 155–164.

Senf, G. M. (1983). The nature and identification of learning disabilities and their relationship to the gifted child. In L. H. Fox, L. Brody, & D. Tobin (Eds.), *Learning disabled/gifted children: Identification and programming.* Baltimore, MD: University Park Press.

Siegel, L. S. & Metsala, J. (1992). An alternative to the food processor approach to subtypes of learning disabilities. In N. N. Singh & I. L. Beale (Eds.), *Learning disabilities: Nature, theory, and treatment* (pp. 44–58). New York, NY: Springer-Verlag.

Sheeber, L. B., Davis, B., Leve, C., Hops, H., & Tildesley, E. (2007). Adolescents' relationships with their mothers and fathers: Associations with depressive disorder and subdiagnostic symptomatology. *Journal of Abnormal Psychology, 116*, 144–154.

Silverman, L. K. (1989). Invisible gifts, invisible handicaps. *Roper Review, 12*, 37–42.

Silverman, L. K. (1993). *Counseling the gifted and talented.* Denver, CO: Love.

Silverman, L. K. (2002). *Upside-down brilliance: The visual-spatial learner.* Denver, CO: DeLeon.

Silverman, L. K. (2003). *Developmental phases of social development.* Retrieved from http://www.sengifted.org/articles_social/Silverman_DevelopmentalPh asesOfSocialDevelopment.shtml

Skrtic, T. M. (1992). *Behind special education: A critical analysis of professional culture and school organization.* Denver, CO: Love.

Sousa, D. A. (2003). *How the gifted brain learns.* Thousand Oaks, CA: Corwin Press.

Spekman, N. J., Goldberg, R. J., & Herman, K. L. (1993). An exploration of risk and resiliency in the lives of individuals with learning disabilities. *Learning Disabilities Research and Practice, 8*, 11–18.

Stein, C. M., Schick, J. H., Taylor, H. G., Shriberg, L. D., Millard, C., Kundtz-Kluge, A., . . . Iyengar, S. K. (2004). Pleiotropic effects of a chromosome 3 locus on speech-sound disorder and reading. *American Journal of Human Genetics, 74*, 283–297.

Sternberg, R. J. (1985). *Beyond IQ: A triarchic theory of human intelligence.* Cambridge, England: Cambridge University Press.

Sternberg, R. J., & Zhang, L. F. (2001). *Perspectives on thinking, learning, and cognitive styles.* Mahwah, NJ: Lawrence Erlbaum.

Sternberg, R. J., Grigorenko, E. L., & Zhang, L. (2008). Styles of learning and thinking matter in instruction and assessment. *Perspectives on Psychological Science, 3*, 486–506.

Stormont, M., Stebbins, M. S., & Holiday, G. (2001). Characteristics and educational support needs of underrepresented gifted adolescents. *Psychology in the Schools, 38*, 413–423.

Tannenbaum, A. J. (1986). Giftedness: A psychosocial approach. In R. J. Sternberg & J. E. Davidson (Eds.), *Conceptions of giftedness* (pp. 21–52). Cambridge, England: Cambridge University Press.

Tannenbaum, A. J., & Baldwin, L. J. (1983). Giftedness and learning disability: A paradoxical combination. In L. H. Fox, L. Brody, & D. Tobin (Eds.),

Learning-disabled/gifted children: Identification and programming (pp. 11–36). Baltimore, MD: University Park Press.

Terman, L. M. (1925). *Genetic studies of genius, Vol. 1: Mental and physical traits of a thousand gifted children.* Stanford, CA: Stanford University Press.

Terman, L. M., & Oden, M. H. (1947). *Genetic studies of genius, Vol. 4: The gifted child grows up.* Stanford, CA: Stanford University Press.

Terman, L. M., & Oden, M. H. (1959). *Genetic studies of genius, Vol. 5: The gifted group at midlife: Thirty-five years' follow-up of a superior group.* Stanford, CA: Stanford University Press.

The Association for the Gifted, Council for Exceptional Children. (2009, Fall). Response to intervention for gifted children. *TAG Update,* 1–3, 6.

Tomlinson, C. A. (1999). *The differentiated classroom: Responding to the needs of all learners.* Alexandria, VA: Association for Supervision and Curriculum Development.

Torrance, E. P. (1981). Implications of whole-brained theories of learning and thinking for computer-based instruction. *Journal of Computer-Based Instruction, 7*(4), 99–105.

Torrance, E. P., & Ball, O. E. (1979). Which gifted students apply what they learn in special programs? *G/C/T, 62,* 7–9.

Trail, B. A. (2006). Parenting twice-exceptional children through frustration to success. *Parenting for High Potential,* 26–30.

Trail, B. A. (2008). *Twice-exceptional learners: What they need in order to thrive* (Unpublished doctoral dissertation). University of Northern Colorado, Greeley, CO.

U.S. Department of Education, Office of Educational Research. (1993). *National excellence: A case for developing America's talent.* Washington, DC: U.S. Government Printing Office.

United States Department of Education, Office of Special Education. (n.d.) *OSEP ideas that work: Tool kit on teaching and assessing students with disabilities.* Retrieved from http://www.osepideasthatwork.org/toolkit/index.asp

Vaidya, S. R. (1993). Gifted children with learning disabilities: Theoretical implications and instructions and instructional challenge. *Education, 113,* 568–574.

VanTassel-Baska, J. (1991). Serving the disabled gifted through educational collaboration. *Journal for the Education of the Gifted, 14,* 246–266.

VanTassel-Baska, J. (2006). A content analysis of evaluation findings across 20 gifted programs: A clarion call for enhanced gifted program development. *Gifted Child Quarterly, 50,* 199–215.

VanTassel-Baska, J., Bass, G., Ries, R., Poland, D., & Avery, L. (1998). A national study of science curriculum effectiveness with high ability students. *Gifted Child Quarterly, 42,* 200–211.

Vaughn, S., & Fuchs, L. S. (2003): Redefining learning disabilities as inadequate response to instruction: The promise and potential problems. *Learning Disabilities Quarterly, 25,* 155–164.

Vellutino, F. R., Fletcher, J. M., Snowling, M. J., & Scanlon, D. M. (2004). Specific reading disability (dyslexia): What have we learned in the past four decades? *Journal of Child Psychology and Psychiatry, 45,* 2–40.

Vespi, L., & Yewchuk, C. (1992). A phenomenological study of the social/emotional characteristics of gifted learning disabled children. *Journal for the Education of the Gifted, 16,* 55–72.

Vygotsky, L. (1978). Interaction between learning and development. In T. M. Cole (Ed.), *Mind in society* (pp. 79–91). Cambridge, MA: Harvard University Press.

Vygotsky, L. (1987). *The collected works of L. S. Vygotsky* (Vol. 1). New York, NY: Plenum.

Waldron, K. A., & Saphire, D. G. (1990). An analysis of WISC-R factors for gifted students with learning disabilities. *Journal of Learning Disabilities, 23,* 491–498.

Waldron, K. A., Saphire, D. G., & Rosenblum, S. A. (1987). Learning disabilities and giftedness: Identification based on self-concept, behavior, and academic patterns. *Journal of Learning Disabilities, 20,* 422–432.

Webb, J. T., Amend, E. R., Webb, N. E., Goerss, J., Beljan, P., & Olenchak, R. (2005). *Misdiagnosis and dual diagnoses of gifted children and adults: ADHD, bipolar, OCD, Asperger's, depression and other disorders.* Scottsdale, AZ: Great Potential Press.

Webb, J. T., Meckstroth, E. A., & Tolan, S. S. (1982). *Guiding the gifted child: A practical source for parents and teachers.* Scottsdale, AZ: Great Potential Press.

Wechsler, D. (2003). *The WISC-IV technical and interpretive manual.* San Antonio, TX: Psychological Corporation.

Weinfeld, R., Barnes-Robinson, L., Jeweler, S., & Shevitz, B. (2002). Academic programs for gifted and talented/learning disabled students. *Roeper Review, 24,* 226–233.

Werner, E. E., & Smith, R. S. (2001). *Journeys from childhood to midlife: Risk, resiliency, and recovery.* New York, NY: Cornell University Press.

Whitmore, J. R. (1980). *Giftedness, conflict, and underachievement.* Boston, MA: Allyn & Bacon.

Whitmore, J. R. (1981). Gifted children with handicapping conditions: A new frontier. *Exceptional Children, 48,* 106–114.

Whitmore, J. R., & Maker, C. J. (1985). *Intellectual giftedness in disabled persons.* Rockville, MD: Aspen Publications.

Whitmore, J. R., Maker, C. J., & Knott, G. (1985). Intellectually gifted persons with specific learning disabilities. In J. R. Whitmore & C. J. Maker (Eds.), *Intellectual giftedness in disabled persons* (pp. 175–206). Rockville, MD: Aspen.

Williams, K. (1988). The learning disabled gifted: An unmet challenge. *Gifted Child Quarterly, 11*, 17–18.

Winne, P. H., Woodlands, M. J., & Wong, B. Y. (1982). Comparability of self-concept among learning disabled, normal, and gifted students. *Journal of Learning Disabilities, 15*, 470–475.

Winner, M. G. (2002). *Inside out: What makes a person with social cognitive deficit tick.* London, England: Jessica Kingsley.

Yewchuck, C. R. (1986). Issues in identification of gifted learning disabled children. *British Columbia: Journal of Special Education, 10*, 201–209.

Yewchuk, C., Delaney, D., Cunningham, J., & Pool, J. (1992). *Teaching gifted/learning disabled students: Case studies and interventions.* Unpublished manuscript, University of Alberta.

Planning Continuum for Helping Twice-Exceptional Gifted Students Succeed

Each of the following pages corresponds with the chapters in the text to allow teachers and administrators to make successful plans for accommodations for twice-exceptional gifted students.

Part I examines how gifted potential should be nurtured. Part II looks at interventions for supporting students' cognitive style. The continuum for Part III allows teachers and administrators to address and encourage students' academic achievement, while the planning pages for Part IV provide strategies to help students foster interpersonal relationships. Finally, Part V of the continuum looks at ways teachers, administrators, and counselors can aid students in promoting their intrapersonal understanding.

As each chapter is read, the continuums that follow can be used to guide planning. Each continuum should be copied and used for individual students. First, check off the guiding principles you wish to address or need to address in more detail. Then, assess each student by noting his or her individual strengths or challenges on a 1–5 scale, with 5 being the highest. After defining the student's needs and setting goals, use the Intervention Continuum checklist on the second half of each planning continuum to select specific interventions you wish to implement. Finally, make notes on who will implement and monitor those interventions and the student's progress. These sheets can then be placed in student's files as a record for future meetings.

Twice-Exceptional Planning Continuum, Part I

Student's Name:	**Date:**

Nurturing Gifted Potential

Guiding Principles:
- ☐ Focus on developing students' strengths and provide opportunities to explore interests.
- ☐ Provide challenging curriculum, relevant learning, and eliminate unnecessary drill and practice.
- ☐ Differentiated instruction to meet their diverse needs:
  - o Content—appropriately challenging
  - o Process—allows students to process information using their preferred style
  - o Product—students use strengths to demonstrate what they have learned
- ☐ Infuse higher order thinking and problem solving
- ☐ Explore the complexity of topics and discuss real-world issues
- ☐ Offer choice in assignments that are relevant, worthwhile, and engaging
- ☐ Provide acceleration options (Most Difficult First, curriculum compacting, subject/grade acceleration)
- ☐ Engage students in pursuing a topic in greater depth and complexity in an independent study

Assessment Data:

Strengths and Challenges:	**Disagree–Agree**
__ Demonstrates advanced ideas and opinions	1__ 2__ 3__ 4__ 5__
__ Has a wide range of interests	1__ 2__ 3__ 4__ 5__
__ Shows a sophisticated vocabulary	1__ 2__ 3__ 4__ 5__
__ Provides penetrating insights	1__ 2__ 3__ 4__ 5__
__ Has superior verbal and communication skills	1__ 2__ 3__ 4__ 5__
__ Displays strong perceptual reasoning skills	1__ 2__ 3__ 4__ 5__
__ Has advanced levels of reasoning and problem solving	1__ 2__ 3__ 4__ 5__
__ Is highly creative, curious, and imaginative	1__ 2__ 3__ 4__ 5__
__ Has a specific talent or consuming interest in _____	1__ 2__ 3__ 4__ 5__

Define Student's Needs:	**SMART Goal:**

Tier			**Interventions:**
1	2	3	

Implementation:
- Who will implement the intervention?
- Where will the intervention occur?
- What is the intervention schedule?
- What resources are needed?

Progress Monitoring:
- Who will monitor the student's progress?
- How will the student's progress be monitored?

Outcomes and Recommendations:

Intervention Continuum to Nurture Gifted Potential

Universal Interventions

- ☐ Instructional planning recognizes and anticipates diverse learning needs of students. Students' strengths, interests, and learning styles guide instruction.
- ☐ Despite their disabilities, twice-exceptional learners may have already mastered grade-level curriculum in their area of strength.
- ☐ Preassess to determine which students need additional challenge. Eliminate unnecessary drill and practice of material already mastered. Use research-based strategies like flexible grouping and Most Difficult First.
- ☐ Differentiate content, process, and product to accommodate diverse needs and learning styles. Provide opportunities for twice-exceptional learners to explore areas of interest in greater depth and complexity. Allow students to use their strengths and preferred learning style to process information and demonstrate what they have learned.
- ☐ Focus on broad-based issues, themes, or problems relevant to the discipline so twice-exceptional learners can investigate real-world issues and develop the habits of mind used by practicing professionals.

Target Interventions

- ☐ Teach students higher order thinking and problem-solving skills needed to interpret major trends and issues, analyze data, synthesize alternative solutions, develop a plan, communicate results, and evaluate the process.
- ☐ Ensure honors and Advanced Placement classes provide the challenging curriculum and faster paced instruction needed to keep students engaged in learning.
- ☐ Provide provisions for progression through the curriculum at the students' learning rates. Curriculum compacting condenses course content and students can use this time to study a topic in greater depth and complexity. They can become a classroom expert and share their knowledge with classmates.
- ☐ Making learning relevant by providing real-world connections increases students' intrinsic motivation. Teach students skills used by practicing professionals.
- ☐ Students who are able to progress through the curriculum at a faster pace need grade acceleration or radical acceleration options so they can complete the K–12 education in a shorter period of time and gain early entrance into college.
- ☐ Magnet classrooms or schools focused on meeting the needs of gifted learners may be appropriate options.

Intensive Interventions

- ☐ Dual enrollment so elementary students can complete middle school classes, middle school students can take high school classes, and high school students can enroll in college courses helps students receive challenging instruction.
- ☐ Afford opportunities to complete independent study projects based on real-world issues. Guide them through the process of identifying issues or problems, using primary and secondary sources to research a topic, design an experiment, collect data, determine results, draw conclusions, and make recommendations.
- ☐ Apprenticeships allow students to gain real-world experiences while mentors can guide students through independent projects. Both are valuable in developing the habits of mind of practicing professionals.

Twice-Exceptional Planning Continuum, Part II

Student's Name: **Date:**

Supporting Cognitive Style

Guiding Principles:

☐ Asynchronous development means cognitive, social, and emotional development is not in sync.

☐ Significant discrepancies between abilities can occur even within the same subject area.

☐ Cognitive processing styles can influence learning, productivity, and achievement.

☐ Students may have deficits in auditory or visual processing, sequential or conceptual thinking, and convergent or divergent thinking that can negatively influence achievement.

☐ Slow processing speed means it takes the students longer to process information and complete assignments.

☐ Executive functioning deficits make it difficult to plan, prioritize, and manage multiple homework assignments.

☐ Gifted students may not be able to sustain attention when the pace of instruction is too slow.

☐ Creative students need assignments that allow them to apply what they have learned in creative ways.

☐ Sensory integration dysfunction means students cannot process sensory information efficiently.

Assessment Data:

Strengths and Challenges:	Disagree–Agree
__ Is a sequential thinker who learns "step-by-step"	1__ 2__ 3__ 4__ 5__
__ Is a conceptual thinker who comprehends the "big picture"	1__ 2__ 3__ 4__ 5__
__ Is unable to think in a sequential, linear fashion	1__ 2__ 3__ 4__ 5__
__ Is an auditory learner who can easily remember verbal information	1__ 2__ 3__ 4__ 5__
__ Is a visual learner who needs to see it to process the information	1__ 2__ 3__ 4__ 5__
__ Demonstrates difficulty following verbal instructions	1__ 2__ 3__ 4__ 5__
__ Shows slow processing speed	1__ 2__ 3__ 4__ 5__
__ Is highly creative and needs to process information in creative ways	1__ 2__ 3__ 4__ 5__
__ Has executive functioning deficits in planning, prioritizing, and organizing	1__ 2__ 3__ 4__ 5__

Define Needs:	SMART Goal:

Tier			Interventions:
1	2	3	

Implementation:
- Who will implement the intervention?
- Where will the intervention occur?
- What is the intervention schedule?
- What resources are needed?

Progress Monitoring:
- Who will monitor the student's progress?
- How will the student's progress be monitored?

Outcomes and Recommendations:

Intervention Continuum for Supporting Cognitive Style

Universal Interventions

☐ Support students with weak auditory processing skills by providing copies of important information like PowerPoint slides and instructions for written assignments.

☐ Present a conceptual overview of the unit and/or lessons so students have a conceptual understanding of information before learning specific details.

☐ Begin discussion or assignment with a divergent brainstorming activity to engage students' creativity and then a convergent activity to select the best solution.

☐ Have students highlight important information while reading to activate their visual memory.

☐ Provide a variety of ways for students to access content information including books, computer programs, audio/video recordings, and highlighted print material.

☐ Use graphic organizers, flow charts, and cognitive webs to guide students' thinking.

☐ Allow students to process the information using their preferred cognitive style. Creative students need to process learning in creative ways.

☐ Provide choice so students can use their preferred style to process information and demonstrate what they have learned.

Target Interventions

☐ Assist students in learning how to listen for key information or provide graphic organizers to complete with important information during lectures.

☐ Provide small-group instruction to develop executive functioning skills in prioritizing, planning, organizing, and time management skills to aid with homework.

☐ Provide preferential seating for students with attention or auditory processing problems and teach attention strategies like sitting up straight and leaning forward toward the speaker.

☐ Utilize technology like speech-activated software, word processing tools, and grammar and spell checkers to increase students' productivity.

☐ Students with slow processing speed need additional time to process information and complete assignments. Monitor students' progress and use the Most Difficult First strategy to reduce the amount of drill and practice assignments accordingly.

☐ Coach students in the use of mnemonics to enhance memory and self-talk to assist auditory learners in processing visual information.

Intensive Interventions

☐ Provide a safe place with cushions or beanbags for students with sensory integration issues to go when they feel overwhelmed.

☐ Monitor students' progress to determine if they are making adequate progress or if they need more intensive interventions.

☐ If students do not respond to targeted interventions, the problem-solving process proceeds to intensive levels of intervention. These interventions provide intensive, systematic individualized or small-group instruction.

☐ A formal, individualized evaluation often begins at this point to determine special education eligibility. Parents are informed of their due process rights and procedural safeguards as required by IDEA 2004 are implemented.

Twice-Exceptional Planning Continuum, Part III

Student's Name:	Date:

Encouraging Academic Achievement

Guiding Principles:

- ☐ Emphasize development of the students' strengths and interests.
- ☐ Utilize continuous assessment to identify skill deficits and provide explicit instruction to improve those skills.
- ☐ Assist students in developing compensatory strategies for areas of weaknesses.
- ☐ Provide short-term accommodations while students are developing skills and learning compensatory strategies
- ☐ Implement strategies to improve fluency and automaticity in reading, writing, and math.
- ☐ Use technology such as word processing tools, spell checkers, and speech recognition software to increase productivity.
- ☐ Engage students in analyzing text as they work to develop basic phonemic awareness and decoding skills.
- ☐ Emphasize the development of problem-solving skills in math rather than computation skills.
- ☐ Allow students to use calculators when solving higher level mathematical problems.

Assessment Data:

Strengths and Challenges:	Disagree–Agree
__ Demonstrates inconsistent or uneven academic skills	1__ 2__ 3__ 4__ 5__
__ Has difficulty expressing feelings or explaining ideas/concept	1__ 2__ 3__ 4__ 5__
__ Hates drill and practice assignments	1__ 2__ 3__ 4__ 5__
__ Avoids school tasks and often fails to complete assignments.	1__ 2__ 3__ 4__ 5__
__ Has poor penmanship and work can be extremely messy	1__ 2__ 3__ 4__ 5__
__ Has problems completing paper and pencil tasks	1__ 2__ 3__ 4__ 5__
__ Appears apathetic, unmotivated, or lacks academic initiative	1__ 2__ 3__ 4__ 5__
__ Has problems with fluency in ( ) writing, ( ) reading, and/or ( ) math	1__ 2__ 3__ 4__ 5__
__ Engages in disruptive or clowning behaviors	1__ 2__ 3__ 4__ 5__
__ Has a high energy level and needs to be actively engaged in learning	1__ 2__ 3__ 4__ 5__

Define Student's Needs:	SMART Goal:

Tier			Interventions:
1	2	3	

Implementation:
- Who will implement the intervention?
- Where will the intervention occur?
- What is the intervention schedule?
- What resources are needed?

Progress Monitoring:
- Who will monitor the student's progress?
- How will the student's progress be monitored?

Outcomes and Recommendations:

Intervention Continuum to Encourage Academic Achievement

Universal Interventions

- ☐ Utilize data from screenings, preassessments, and skill assessments to guide instruction and to determine which students are at risk.
- ☐ Strive to provide instruction at an appropriate level to prevent boredom when students are not challenged or frustration when the challenge level is too high and they do not have the skills necessary to be successful.
- ☐ Differentiate instruction to meet their diverse needs
  - o Content—utilize multiple sources for accessing information
  - o Process—use graphic organizers to aid students in processing information
  - o Product—allow choice in assignments making sure they are relevant and engaging with connections to real-world problems

Target Interventions

- ☐ Realize that even though students are gifted, they may experience learning difficulties. Use an encouraging empathic approach and support twice-exceptional learners as they strive to develop skills in deficit areas.
- ☐ Grouping of students should be flexible so twice-exceptional learners have access to high-level, challenging instruction as well as remedial instruction.
- ☐ Continue to focus on the development of the students' strengths along with emphasis on developing higher order thinking and problem-solving skills even though the students are struggling to develop basic skills in reading, writing, and math.
- ☐ Timely interventions are necessary for reducing the risk of frustrated students developing social and emotional issues. Make sure students experience more success each day than struggles.
- ☐ Use diagnostic assessments to identify deficit areas and provide explicit research-based instruction to teach necessary skill. Refer to interventions suggested under the headings of dyslexia, dysgraphia, and dyscalculia.
- ☐ Help students to understand why it is important to improve deficit skills. Fluency and automaticity are issues for many twice-exceptional learners. They need to learn how to develop realistic short-term personal goals and persist to achieve those goals.
- ☐ Monitor students' progress to determine if they are making adequate progress or if they need more intensive interventions.

Intensive Interventions

- ☐ Begin the collaborative problem-solving process when the students first begin to struggle to prevent students from experiencing significant failure. Make sure the classroom teacher has support from both gifted and special education.
- ☐ If students do not respond to targeted interventions, the problem-solving process proceeds to intensive levels of intervention. These interventions provide intensive, systematic, individualized or small-group instruction.
- ☐ A formal, individualized evaluation often begins at this point to determine special education eligibility. Parents are informed of their due process rights and procedural safeguards as required by IDEA 2004 are implemented.

Twice-Exceptional Planning Continuum, Part IV
Student's Name: **Date:**
Fostering Interpersonal Relationships

Guiding Principles:

- ☐ Provide opportunities for students to work with peers who have similar abilities and interests.
- ☐ Identify students with inadequate social skills, poor peer relationships, or difficulties with authoritarian figures.
- ☐ Introverted students need time to recharge after group activities, while extroverts gain strength from interactions.
- ☐ Guard against peer bullying and anti-intellectual climates in classrooms and schools.
- ☐ Work collaboratively with parents and students to develop a comprehensive plan for intervention.
- ☐ Empower twice-exceptional learners by teaching them the skills they need to achieve their potential.
- ☐ Teach self-advocacy skills and practice these skills in a safe environment.
- ☐ Supportive, flexible teachers are needed to encourage students' efforts to become successful learners.
- ☐ Invite students to participate in friendship groups to learn the skills needed to establish and maintain friendships.
- ☐ Encourage students to participate in extracurricular and community activities.

Assessment Data:

Strengths and Challenges:	**Disagree–Agree**
__ Is an introvert who needs time to recharge and reflect	1__ 2__ 3__ 4__ 5__
__ Is an extrovert who is energized by being around others	1__ 2__ 3__ 4__ 5__
__ Demonstrates poor social skills and exhibits antisocial behaviors	1__ 2__ 3__ 4__ 5__
__ Has difficulty with peer relationships/bullied by peers	1__ 2__ 3__ 4__ 5__
__ Has strained relationships with family members	1__ 2__ 3__ 4__ 5__
__ Is empowered by parents	1__ 2__ 3__ 4__ 5__
__ Is enabled by parents	1__ 2__ 3__ 4__ 5__
__ Is withdrawn and is becoming increasingly isolated	1__ 2__ 3__ 4__ 5__
__ Has affiliations with others through extracurricular activities or clubs	1__ 2__ 3__ 4__ 5__
__ Shows development of leadership skills	1__ 2__ 3__ 4__ 5__

Define Student's Needs:	**SMART Goals:**

Tier			Interventions:
1	2	3	

Implementation:
- Who will implement the intervention?
- Where will the intervention occur?
- What is the intervention schedule?
- What resources are needed?

Progress Monitoring:
- Who will monitor the student's progress?
- How will the student's progress be monitored?

Outcomes and Recommendations:

Intervention Continuum to Foster Interpersonal Relationships

Universal Interventions

- ☐ Screening, systematic assessment, and progress monitoring are important for identifying students who are having problems with personal relationships.
- ☐ Provide a learning environment that values individual differences and honors diversity.
- ☐ Give students opportunities to work with peers with similar interests and abilities.
- ☐ Encourage students to become involved in school clubs and community activities.
- ☐ Enthusiastic teachers who are flexible and supportive are needed to encourage students to develop their potential and overcome their disability.
- ☐ Guard against peer bullying and anti-intellectual climates in schools.
- ☐ Encourage feelings of empathy and do not tolerate intolerance.
- ☐ Refer students who are showing signs of isolation for group counseling
- ☐ Clearly state and consistently implement expectations and consequences.
- ☐ Search for opportunities to encourage appropriate social interactions for socially challenged students.

Target Interventions

- ☐ Preselect groups and do not allow students to choose or reject others.
- ☐ Invite students to join friendship groups where they can learn social skills needed to develop peer relationships and maintaining friendships.
- ☐ Assist families in learning how to empower their children to use their strengths and overcome their weaknesses verses enabling children to use their disability as an excuse.
- ☐ Coach students in understanding body language and reading social cues.
- ☐ Help students learn how to resolve issues in friendships.
- ☐ Provide opportunities for students to learn self-advocacy skills and use role-play for students to practice.
- ☐ Teach students the skills they need to be able to participate in collaborative work.
- ☐ Provide explicit instruction to help students improve relationships with peers, teachers, and family.

Intensive Interventions

- ☐ Teach students the skills they need to become self-advocates.
- ☐ Teach leadership skills and provide in-school leadership opportunities.
- ☐ Facilitate mentorships and/or apprenticeships.
- ☐ Specialized counseling is necessary to assist students in dealing with intensities, sensitivities, feelings of being different, and isolation.
- ☐ Provide support services for students with a trained counselor, psychologist, or social worker.
- ☐ Develop a behavior plan to address problem situations.

Twice-Exceptional Planning Continuum, Part V

Student's Name:	Date:

Promoting Intrapersonal Understanding

Guiding Principles:

- ☐ Identify students with emotional issues such as low self-esteem, dysfunctional perfectionism, unrealistic expectations, anxiety, and/or depression.
- ☐ Assist students in understanding and accepting their strengths, weaknesses, and cognitive styles.
- ☐ Teach perfectionists that mistakes are a part of the learning process.
- ☐ Promote success as the result of effort, not ability.
- ☐ Help students deal with sensitivity, intensity, and/or emotionality.
- ☐ Teach students emotional self-regulation skills, metacognitive scripts, and emotional problem solving.
- ☐ Stress can result in internalized or externalized behaviors.
- ☐ Coach students in setting realistic goals and celebrate successful achievement of goals.
- ☐ Self-esteem increases when student are able to achieve their goals.

Assessment Data:

Strengths and Challenges:	Disagree–Agree
__ Is highly sensitive to criticism	1__ 2__ 3__ 4__ 5__
__ Is a perfectionist and afraid to risk making mistakes	1__ 2__ 3__ 4__ 5__
__ Gets easily frustrated and tend to give up quickly on difficult tasks	1__ 2__ 3__ 4__ 5__
__ Blames others for mistakes or problems	1__ 2__ 3__ 4__ 5__
__ Relates success to "luck" or "ability"	1__ 2__ 3__ 4__ 5__
__ Believes success is achieved through "hard work" and "effort"	1__ 2__ 3__ 4__ 5__
__ Is self-critical and has low self-esteem	1__ 2__ 3__ 4__ 5__
__ Suffers from anxiety and/or depression	1__ 2__ 3__ 4__ 5__
__ Has a high level of personal understanding and acceptance	1__ 2__ 3__ 4__ 5__
__ Holds realistic expectations	1__ 2__ 3__ 4__ 5__

Define Student's Needs:	SMART Goals:

Tier			Interventions:
1	2	3	

Implementation:
- Who will implement the intervention?
- Where will the intervention occur?
- What is the intervention schedule?
- What resources are needed?

Progress Monitoring:
- Who will monitor the student's progress?
- How will the student's progress be monitored?

Outcomes and Recommendations:

	Intervention Continuum to Promote Intrapersonal Understanding
Universal Interventions	☐ Screen and systematically assess students to identify those who have low self-esteem, dysfunctional perfectionism, unrealistic expectations, anxiety, or depression.
	☐ Focus attention on the development of potential rather than trying to fix students.
	☐ Create a classroom environment that values individual differences and fosters appreciation of the diverse qualities of all learners.
	☐ Promote the development of positive self-esteem by providing the appropriate level of challenge where students can be successful.
	☐ Clearly state and consistently implement expectations and consequences.
	☐ Help students understand that mistakes are part of the learning experience.
	☐ Promote understanding that success is a result of effort rather than ability.
	☐ Schedule breaks for physical activity to reduce mental fatigue.
	☐ Maximize success and minimize failures.
Target Interventions	☐ Provide opportunities for students to work with intellectual peers and with peers who have similar interests.
	☐ Facilitate the development of personal awareness, understanding, and acceptance.
	☐ Use hypothetical situations, bibliotherapy, and moral dilemmas to foster an accepting environment for all students.
	☐ Facilitate group-building activities and development of empathy in students.
	☐ Utilize a grading rubric and guide students in evaluating their own work.
	☐ Coach students in learning to set realistic long-term goals and to break goals down into manageable short-term goals.
	☐ Celebrate attainment of individual goals and self-actualization.
	☐ Avoid power struggles, pick your battles, and maintain a calm, neutral response.
	☐ Provide career exploration and career counseling programs to assist students in planning for their future.
	☐ Facilitate students in the development of self-regulation, locus of control, and attainment of personal goals.
Intensive Interventions	☐ Promote and teach students positive coping strategies such as seeking support, positive reappraisal, and accepting responsibility.
	☐ Teach mental scripts that emphasize self-regulation so students can learn to manage their anger and behavior.
	☐ Teach students how to label, control, and express their emotions appropriately.
	☐ Provide specialized counseling for students who are exhibiting signs of anxiety, dysfunctional perfectionism, depression, stress, or suicide.
	☐ Use mentorships and apprenticeships with expert practitioners and gifted role models so students will learn the habits of mind of practicing professionals.

Twice-Exceptional Education Plan

Student's Name: **Date:**

Strengths:	Challenges:	Preferences:

Nurturing Gifted Potential

Define Gifted Needs:	SMART Goal:

Tier	Interventions:
1 2 3	

Supporting Cognitive Style

Define Cognitive Needs:	SMART Goal:

Tier	Interventions:
1 2 3	

Encouraging Academic Achievement

Define Academic Needs:	SMART Goal:

Tier	Interventions:
1 2 3	

Fostering Interpersonal Relationships

Define Interpersonal Needs:	SMART Goal:

Tier	Interventions:
1 2 3	

Promoting Intrapersonal Understanding

Define Intrapersonal Needs:	SMART Goal:

Tier	Interventions:
1 2 3	

Twice-Exceptional Education Plan	
Student's Name:	**Date:**
Implementation	
Who will implement the intervention?	**What resources are needed?**
Where will the intervention occur?	**When is the intervention schedule?**
Progress Monitoring	
Who will monitor the student's progress?	**How will the student's progress be monitored?**
Outcomes	
Recommendations	

ABOUT THE AUTHOR

Beverly A. Trail, Ed.D, is the National Association for Gifted Children's Special Population Network Chair. She is a twice-exceptional consultant, trainer, researcher, and frequent presenter at the National Association for Gifted Children and Council for Exceptional Children conventions. Dr. Trail earned a doctorate in special education from the University of Northern Colorado, a master's degree in gifted education from the University of Denver, and endorsement as a Gifted Education Specialist. Currently, she is developing and teaching courses in a new master's degree program for gifted education at Regis University.

Her career in education spans 22 years, with experience at the district level as gifted education coordinator, resource teacher, and twice-exceptional consultant. The school-based gifted program she coordinated was designated as a model program in gifted education by the Colorado Department of Education 2+2 Excellence in Education Project. She was contracted by Colorado Department of Education to develop an introductory resource handbook and training module for the Twice-Exceptional Project. For 3 years, she conducted twice-exceptional trainings throughout the state. As a result of her extensive work in gifted education, she was inducted into the Colorado Academy of Educators for the Gifted, Talented, and Creative.